NEW ZEALAND
A PERSONAL DISCOVERY

DICK PARSONS

Copyright © 2018 by Dick Parsons
All rights reserved. No part of this book may be reproduced, scanned,
or distributed in any printed or electronic form without permission.
First Edition: December 2018
Printed in the United States of America
ISBN: 1642542342
ISBN: 9781642542349

Table of Contents

Acknowledgements vii

Chapter One 1
Chapter Two 9
Chapter Three 20
Chapter Four 28
Chapter Five 35
Chapter Six 48
Chapter Seven 65
Chapter Eight 79
Chapter Nine 89
Chapter Ten 105
Chapter Eleven 110
Chapter Twelve 121
Chapter Thirteen 128
Chapter Fourteen 137
Chapter Fifteen 150
Chapter Sixteen 161
Chapter Seventeen 171
Chapter Eighteen 178

Bibliography 189
New Zealand 191

Acknowledgements

To Clare and Pat for their great kindness and enthusiastic help, to my patient and supportive wife Anne, and to all those friendly Kiwis we met along the way.

ALSO BY THE SAME AUTHOR
A FISHER OF SLAVES AND
TURBANS

A FAMILY DIVIDED

Chapter One

THE GIFT OF THE SEA

NEW ZEALAND

Our Boeing 747 touched down with a reassuring thud and a squeal of tyres as we landed at Auckland International Airport. We had travelled halfway round the world from our home in England and at last we had arrived in New Zealand, the most distant of all dominions, who without hesitation had come to Britain's aid in two world wars, not for any economic or strategic reasons, but for family ties and loyalty to the British crown.

I had wanted to visit New Zealand for over forty years, and when I was young I had volunteered for exchange service with the Royal New Zealand Navy. Unfortunately it was not to be, but the desire to see the country and its people had lingered and now it was to be realised and I was to make my own voyage of discovery.

Before the speed and regularity of air travel made the world smaller, New Zealand was incredibly remote. It is made up of three islands: the North Island; the South Island, the biggest; and in the extreme south, Stewart Island, the smallest. Situated roughly midway between the equator and the South Pole it is isolated in the vast Pacific Ocean. Dwarfed by its neighbour the continent of Australia some 1,200 miles to the west, it is larger than Britain and its climate varies from sub-tropical in the north to temperate in the south.

In prehistoric times it was uninhabited by man; neither were there any other mammals, and much of its native flora remains unique, as does the national emblem, the kiwi, one of many birds thought to have been blown onto the islands. With no predators to hunt them, kiwis abandoned flight and walked in search of food, and their wings atrophied to small stumps.

No one knows when man first arrived, but it is now thought that he arrived from East Polynesia some time in the eighth century. These early settlers have been called the Moa-hunters. The moa, which is now extinct, was a huge flightless bird somewhat like an ostrich. Unused to the presence of humans and other predators it must have been an easy prey and a good source of food. Little seems to be known about the Moa-hunters. They used the bones of the moa for tools and decoration and they were a stone-age, fishing and hunting people. There is also evidence of man-made soils fertilised with wood ash and loosened by added gravel, which leads us to the conclusion that they practised some form of agriculture. Many pits of varying shapes and sizes have been discovered on sites believed to have been occupied by the Moa-hunters, and it seems these were probably storage pits for their crops.

The Maoris came later, probably some time in the fourteenth century. Legend has it that the islands were discovered early in the tenth century by a man called Kupe, who originated from a place called

Hawaiki. On his return he gave directions for reaching this new and distant land, which he called *Tiritiri o te moana*, the Gift of the Sea. A legendary fleet of canoes under the leadership of Toi subsequently set out without compass or chart to sail the vast spaces of the Pacific Ocean to find and populate the new land.

Whether there is any truth in this, or indeed where Hawaiki was, no one knows. Some evidence based mainly on the similarities of language suggests that Hawaiki may have been Tahiti; while some points to the Marquesas Islands. But many think that the arrival of the Maoris in their famous canoes was a more haphazard affair, with Polynesians setting off on short voyages, but being blown off course and landing in New Zealand by accident.

We shall never know, as the Maoris had no written language and all their history was handed down by word of mouth, so legends and myths abound and facts are rare. Several attempts have been made to write an authoritative history of these early colonists and perhaps the most detailed is *The Coming of the Maoris*, written in 1949 by Sir Peter Buck, a Member of Parliament and Minister of Maori Affairs.

The first European to sight New Zealand was Abel Janszoon Tasman, the greatest of Dutch navigators. Born at Lutjegast in Gröningen, the most northerly of the Dutch provinces, he served many years as a captain in the service of the Dutch East India Company. He sailed in August 1642 from Batavia, now Djakarta, the capital city of Indonesia, with two vessels, the *Heemskerk* and the *Zeehaen*, in search of the great South Land, which we now know as Australia. Various sightings of this land had been made during voyages dating from 1605. Sailing south via Mauritius and then turning eastwards with the Roaring Forties, Tasman sighted land on 24th November that year. He named this Van Diemen's Land, after Anthoonij van Diemen, the Governor-General of the Dutch East Indies who had sent him out to explore the coast of this southern continent. Perhaps this was a mark of respect for his employer or perhaps it was to ensure his future, but the name did not last and we now know this land as Tasmania.

Leaving Tasmania, he planned to visit the Solomon Islands, but on 13th December he discovered a "high mountainous country" which he called Staten Landt, i.e. Land of the States, that is the States of Holland. He thought this was part of a great Antarctic continent linking up with what we now call Chile, but now we know it was the west coast of the South Island of New Zealand. On December 18th he anchored at the entrance of a "wide opening", which he took to be a "fine bay", which is now known as Cook Strait. The next day the ships were visited by men from shore in two canoes. They called out "in a rough, hollow voice" and blew on an instrument, which was probably a large shell. Their skin seemed to be coloured yellowish brown and they wore their hair on top of their heads and decorated it with a large white feather. Tasman sent a boat out to make friends with these strange people, but the Maoris rammed it and in this first encounter between Maori and European four Dutchmen were killed. Despite musket shot from the Dutch ships the Maoris withdrew to shore without apparent loss.

Tasman named this spot *Moordenaars* ('Murderers') Bay and weighed anchor and left. He charted the west coast of the North Island, before returning to Batavia where it was decided to rename this inhospitable land Nieuw Zeeland after the Dutch Province.

And so the Maoris had a further interlude of some 127 years' undisturbed occupation of their land until the arrival of Captain James Cook in the barque *Endeavour*. The son of a Yorkshire farm bailiff, he was apprenticed at an early age to Messrs Walker, ship owners at Whitby. He served in the Norway, Baltic and Newcastle trades and when in 1755 he had risen to become a mate he joined the Royal Navy. Soon he was to become a specialist in surveying and was actively engaged in surveying the St Lawrence river prior to General Wolfe's famous attack on Quebec.

In the mid-1760s astronomers were eagerly looking forward to the transit of Venus across the face of the sun. This was due to occur in 1769 and would not take place again for another hundred years. It was an important event as it could be used to determine the distance of the earth from the sun. But to do so it was necessary to take observations at widely separated points on the surface of the earth. The Royal Society wanted to send a scientific expedition to the South Seas to observe the transit and the Admiralty was instructed to provide a suitable vessel to observe the phenomenon in Tahiti, predicted to occur on 3rd June 1769.

At the age of forty, Cook, who was held in high esteem as a mathematician and surveyor was appointed to lead this expedition. He was commissioned as a Lieutenant and given command of the Endeavour. The Endeavour was a barque of 370 tons formerly employed as a collier, which was fitted out for the expedition at the personal expense of an eminent English naturalist Joseph Banks, later to be knighted, who also embarked on the expedition. Cook observed the transit at Tahiti as instructed and then opened sealed orders which had been given to him before he left Plymouth in August the year before. These instructed him to make such discoveries of new lands as would "redound greatly to the honour of this nation". He was ordered to proceed southward and search for the vast continent, which was widely held to exist somewhere to the south of Tahiti. His search was to be conducted to the east of Tasman's Nieuw Zeeland between the latitudes of 35 and 40 degrees South.

Before the expedition left Tahiti, Cook took on board Tupia, a chieftain and the principal priest of the local religion. He had picked up a little English in the two years since these strange white men in their great ships had visited his islands and it was hoped that he would be able to help the British communicate more easily with the local inhabitants of any land they might discover.

On Saturday 7th October 1769, Endeavour's masthead lookout reported land and on the Monday the ship was able to sail into a bay and anchor in the entrance of a small river. Cook and some of his men rowed themselves ashore in two boats, where they could see some natives and, in the distance, their huts. But when they tried to land, one of their boats was attacked and in the ensuing struggle a native was killed. Cook and his men retired to the Endeavour. They tried to make friendly contact again the next day with some canoes in the bay and they found that Tupia could indeed converse with them, but again they were attacked. In the fighting three natives fell into the water and were rescued by Cook's men and taken back to the Endeavour. Here according to Cook's log "they were clothed and treated with all imaginable kindness and to the surprise of everybody became at once as cheerful and as merry as if they had been with their own friends".

The next day Cook intended to land his three captives and while his men were ashore cutting wood he made contact again with the locals. This time Tupia and the three captives tried to convince them of Cook's good intentions, and at last some friendly though hesitant contact was made; but the three Maoris rescued from the sea the day before refused to stay ashore.

The next day, Wednesday 11th, the three natives, who had by now taken to the Endeavour, were persuaded to leave and the ship sailed from the bay, which Cook named Poverty Bay "because it afforded us no one thing we wanted".

So ended the first contact between the Maoris and the British: not a very auspicious start and it is not difficult to imagine the fear, suspicion and downright awe which the sight of this huge ship and its crew must have aroused in the minds and hearts of the Maoris. Many years later a Maori chief named Te Horeta Taniwha (Red Dragon) recalled, as a small boy, seeing the Endeavour come into Mercury Bay. He said the villagers watching the crew lower a boat and row to the shore thought the new arrivals were some kind of goblins, with eyes at the backs of their heads; for if not, how could they face the opposite direction to that in which they were going? He remembered their astonishment and terror when one of these white men pointed a stick at a bird and there was a crack of thunder and a flash of lightning and the bird fell dead. The strange creatures, he said, were kind to the children and one of them patted him on the head and gave him a nail, which he kept and revered as an object of worship for the rest of his life.

Cook spent the next five months circumnavigating and charting the coasts and bays of both islands before setting off on the long return voyage home, which ended when he presented his journal and charts to King George III. His chart of New Zealand was published on 1st January 1772 and was remarkably accurate, though it shows South Cape as part of the South Island and the existence of Stewart Island was not recorded. He was saddened by his reception at Poverty Bay, which is on the east coast of the North Island north of Hawke Bay, but he met a different reception some two weeks later. Endeavour anchored a little further north in Tolaga Bay, on 23rd October, and here the natives were "to all appearance not only very friendly but ready to traffic", and Cook and his crew were able to get fresh water from the stream and wood and "Sellery and Scurvy grass". The natives also sold them fish and as time went by relations with the natives improved and Cook came to respect them as "a brave, warlike people, with sentiments void of treachery".

Other explorers followed in Cook's wake. The Frenchman De Surville came two months after Cook. His brutal treatment of the natives led to the massacre of his countryman Marion du Fresne three years later. Spanish and Italian expeditions also followed and knowledge of this new land began to spread.

In the last decade of the eighteenth century a vessel left a gang of sealers at Dusky Sound on the south west coast of the South Island and at about the same time vessels began fishing for sperm whales in New Zealand waters. The Fancy from Sydney spent three months in the Hauraki Gulf, to the east of present day Auckland, collecting timber for spars. These early commercial ventures were soon copied, and within ten years British, French and American whalers were fishing regularly in these waters and the hunting for seals led to the indiscriminate slaughter of bulls, cows and pups on the shores of the South Island.

These activities began to bring the local tribes into frequent contact with Europeans and regular visits began to be made by ships from Sydney. Maoris helped to cut timber and drag the great trunks down to the sea and load them onto the ships. Flax was another item sought by the Europeans. Gradually a busy trade sprang up. The Maoris wanted nails, which could be fashioned into fish hooks, and other iron tools far superior to their own stone age ones. In exchange they provided women and fresh food.

Traders were quick to seize the opportunities for profit and ships started anchoring in New Zealand waters not only to bring the newfound resources back to New South Wales, but also to kidnap the natives for crew. A prison chaplain who encountered these tattooed Maori seamen in Sydney determined to save them and their people from paganism and exploitation; so industry and commerce brought missionaries, in their wake.

Thus this sleeping land which Maui, the youngest of five brothers in Polynesian myth, fished up out of the ocean depths, was moulded by exploitation, wars and the gospel into this beautiful and productive land we were about to explore.

Chapter Two

CITY OF SAILS

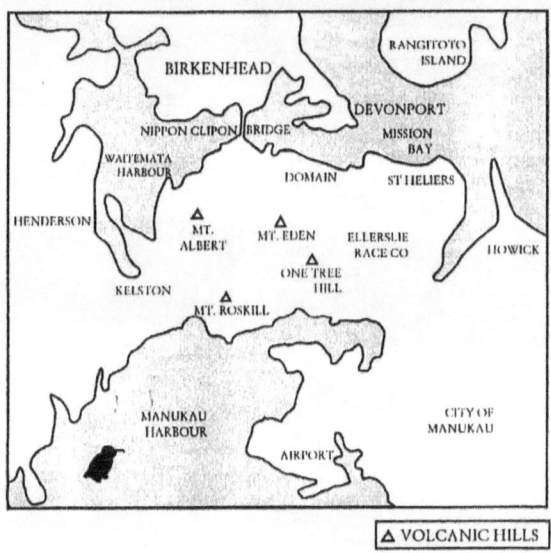

AUCKLAND

Having read a little about the discovery and development of the country, we felt it was now time to start on our own exploration. Though we lacked a stick that would miraculously issue forth thunder and lightning, we did have our own Tupia in the shape of our very good friends, who met us at the airport. They soon whisked us off to their house just above St Helier's Bay overlooking Tamaki Strait and Rangitoto in the distance with its volcanic cone reaching to the sky and forming part of the great panoramic view which the Aucklanders seem to take for granted. Rangitoto was the last of the city's 48 volcanoes to erupt, some 250 years ago, but now stands serene and aloof, content with its lovely symmetrical shade. Auckland is called the City of Sails and it is a very apt name for we seemed to have a never-ending procession of yachts and dinghies parading before our eyes; and with the commercial harbour at Waitemata away to our left, there was always plenty of movement on the water to keep one's eyes busy absorbing this beautiful view.

We had arrived in early February to escape the winter in England and to enjoy three summers in succession. Not that Auckland has much winter by our standards, as the huge geraniums which had survived many local winters testified. Theirs is a very likeable climate, not really too hot in the summer, and frost is a rarity. In fact we learnt that the winters are not cold enough for daffodils and narcissi to grow here, though they do well in the South Island.

We enjoyed a refreshing dip in the swimming pool before tea in the garden and felt welcome and relaxed. Over tea we discussed itineraries, hotels and the hiring of cars and were offered books on f lora and fauna. We were also invited to go with our friends in their car to Lake Taupo, and stay with them for a few days in their cottage on the water's edge before we went solo.

But first we had to see Auckland. The city, the largest in the country with a population of about a million, sits astride a narrow isthmus only about two or three miles wide at its narrowest point. This narrow strip of land separates two seas, the Pacific Ocean and the commercial harbour at Waitemata to the east and the Tasman Sea with the airport jutting out into Manakau harbour to the west. The area - which includes seven extinct volcanoes - has even from the earliest of times been densely populated, no doubt because of its easy access by sea, and the natural defensive position offered by the volcanoes, on many of which one can see the signs of ancient fortifications.

Not the present capital city nor the first, Auckland was chosen as the site of Government in March 1841 by the Lieutenant-Governor William Hobson when it had become apparent that Russell, the capital of only ten months standing, was too remote for the governance of this long and narrow country. He named the city in honour of his patron, the Earl of Auckland, then the Viceroy of India. At that time the native population had been decimated by epidemics and inter-tribal warfare and the site was practically deserted; but since its inception the city has grown rapidly, though haphazardly, with European and Maori coexisting. But the Maori wars in the 1860s and 70s created great tensions and the development slowed, and in 1865 the seat of government was transferred once more, this time to Wellington, an even more centrally placed location from which to govern this country divided geographically by the Cook Strait. In 1963 the Auckland Regional Authority was established to co-ordinate planning and development, and today Auckland is the largest and most multicultural of all the cities in New Zealand. In fact it claims to have the largest Polynesian population in the world.

Now it is a thoroughly modern city with museums, art galleries, theatres and cinemas, plenty of hotels, restaurants by the score and of course being populated by outdoor people it has masses of sporting facilities. It even has its own race course and with memories of having a f lutter on the horses years ago on one of her earlier travels, my wife wanted to renew her acquaintance with the beautifully maintained course at Ellerslie. Regrettably there was no opportunity for her to repeat her earlier financial dealings with the bookies, but at least she was able to satisfy her nostalgic desires and we came away neither richer nor poorer!

I was keen that we should pay a homage to One Tree Hill. What an intriguing name that is: One Tree Hill! Sure enough, there on the summit of this extinct volcano is a windswept, weather-beaten and lonely pine tree. We drove through Cornwall Park and up the tree-lined drive, passing masochists jogging uphill, and arrived fresh as daisies at the top. There in the shadow of this lofty tree we had a fabulous view of the city below us, with all the other volcanoes, the two harbours, the airport and across the straits to the east Rangitoto standing solitary and majestic.

Close by the tree and even overshadowing it on One Tree Hill is an obelisk, about 70 feet tall, built to honour Kupe. Carving at the base of the monument states that he was the first known Maori to visit these islands and that he did so in 925 AD. It also commemorates the first legendary emigration from Hawaiki in 1350 of the fleet of seven canoes after whom the main Maori tribes are named, Tainui, Arawa, Mata-Atua, Aotea, Takitumu, Horouta and Tokomaru. The tablet also remembers the signing of the Treaty of Waitangi, by which the tribes accepted the sovereignty of the British Crown in the person of Queen Victoria. So there you have the condensed history of this country, conjectural perhaps, but nevertheless carved in a tablet of stone. What can be more convincing than that!

Avid for more views of the city, in the comfort of our car we climbed another cone. This time Mount Eden, perhaps at 643 feet not quite so high as One Tree Hill, but nevertheless offering further panoramic views. Just before the summit we passed a deep red lava crater, thought to have been an ancient Maori Pa, that is a Maori fortified village. No Maoris live here now and the only inhabitants were sheep grazing contentedly on this historic site.

By now we were hooked on these gentle mountains and soon we were climbing Mount Savage at the summit of which is a memorial to the first Labour Prime Minister, Micky Savage. In the 1935 elections his party easily defeated its opponents and in a tremendous burst of legislative activity he transformed the country into a Welfare State. Arbitration between employers and trades unions was to be compulsory, a minimum wage for all workers was set and a large public works programme was set in train to reduce the level of unemployment. Pensions and family allowances were all increased and housing was built to be let at low rental. But his greatest achievement was the introduction of a national Health Service to provide medicines, medical treatment and maternity benefit. It was the first comprehensive and integrated system of social security in the world. The memorial was built by a grateful nation and the site named after him. The garden which surrounds his memorial was a swathe of colour with petunias, begonias, pansies and a host of other flowers which almost overwhelmed the stonework of the paths and terraces.

Here on the side of the hill was the first Maori habitation we had so far seen: a small area claimed by the Maoris has been reserved for them. Sad to say it looked a bit like 'set-aside' land in UK, with little obvious signs of cultivation. Nor did we see any Maori buildings, not a Meeting House in sight and not one Maori carving was visible. Just a few little wooden houses that one might see anywhere. Clearly we would have to wait a little longer before we saw the real thing.

Our hosts drove us through the Auckland Domain, a large expanse of parkland almost in the centre of the city, with beautiful trees, formal gardens and a complex of glasshouses containing a collection of tropical plants. It is also the site of the Auckland War Memorial Museum, which remembers the dead of two World Wars and has the names of all the battles in which the New Zealand armed services have fought, engraved at the top of the columns on the outer wall of this magnificent building. In front stands the cenotaph which forms the centrepiece of the annual memorial service to honour those who fell in the two World Wars and also on Anzac day to remember those killed in that disastrous campaign at Gallipoli in the 1914–18 war.

Inside, the museum has a large number of displays, but the most important is the huge collection of Maori art. A great carved meeting house and the only surviving Maori war canoe are centrepieces of the display. Both are impressive, but the canoe at 82 feet long dominates the room and together they are statements of a powerful and highly organised society. I particularly liked the model of a Maori Pa, which showed how a village was protected by earthworks and palisades made from the ponga tree, still widespread and used to this day for fencing. Before the Europeans arrived the Maoris lived in the stone age and their weapons were mostly wooden, but like the canoe and meeting house finely carved. How did they do this? There were some f lint tools to be seen, but their most important material for toolmaking was pounamu, which is better known as greenstone and has the appearance of jade. Not only is it a beautiful material with its lovely translucent colouring, but it is also extremely hard and can be shaped to a fine edge. In one of the display cases we saw a huge piece of greenstone fashioned into a blade for an adze and of course it was with adzes such as this that they cut down the great trees and hollowed them to make the huge war canoes. No wonder they went to great lengths to find this green stone. Other displays showed how flax was woven to make mats, clothing and even sails and how the flax cloaks for the Chief and his entourage were covered with feathers taken from birds they trapped. And before I had to leave to join my companions, I spied in the corner a model double- hulled canoe, with its centrally placed thatched cabin. I wondered how truly it represented those seven canoes whose names are inscribed on that lofty obelisk.

Our route home lead past the Holy Trinity cathedral, built in red brick in 1973 and now being extended in a modern style reminiscent of the new shopping centres which spring up on the outskirts of towns in the UK! It was built to replace the earlier wooden church of St Mary's, which was to be demolished and its site sold. Thankfully however, after much campaigning the church was saved, but had to be moved physically across the road to its present position alongside the new Cathedral. In UK we really aren't used to buildings moving across the street, but our hosts thought this was a fairly routine thing and, as we were to learn, it seems to happen all the time. In fact one can buy a house with a low bungalow between it and a lovely view of the harbour only to find at a later date that the nice little bungalow between you and the sea gets up and moves during the night, and that a few days later some large two-storeyed house arrives in its place! End of nice view and start of bad neighbourly relations! However, whether St Mary's is on one side of the street or the other, it is a beautiful gothic style church built of native woods and tastefully painted in a Wedgwood blue with white window frames. How I longed to go in and explore this gem, but vandals are international and the building was locked.

Nearing home we drove along the coast road overlooking Tamaki Strait and around Mission Bay, so called because this was where the house for the missionaries was built. The sturdy stone building still stands, but is now used as a restaurant. We continued to St Helier's Bay along a very pleasant scenic road with native pohutukawa trees lining our route. The pohutukawa is also called the Christmas tree as in December its silvery buds burst and for a week or two its sombre foliage is lost in a mantle of crimson blossom. Each flower is full of nectar and on a warm day the tree becomes alive with birds and bees enjoying the feast. Though we were there in mid-January we were lucky enough to see some late blossom and it made us realise what a splendid sight we would have seen, had we come a few weeks earlier.

Too much sightseeing is exhausting and we were beginning to feel the need to recharge our batteries with a good meal. St Helier's is an attractive waterside suburb with restaurants a-plenty. Not only all the European varieties, but Indian, Chinese, Vietnamese and others, which reflect the make up of the population. Few restaurants in New Zealand are licensed to sell alcohol, so having purchased our own bottle of wine from a nearby off-licence, we chose a restaurant. We think this is a very good idea as one can have the wine of one's choice without the enormous mark-up which restaurants certainly charge in the UK. In fact I don't believe we were charged corkage, but with the welcome given us by the proprietor and the charm of his waitress I can't really remember!

Remembering my unsuccessful attempt to serve on exchange with the RNZN, I wanted to see the Naval Base, which is at Devonport on the northern side of Waitemata harbour, and so off we set. Until the late 50s, vehicles could only cross the harbour by means of a ferry, which was just not up to the job. Back in the early 30s various plans for a bridge or tunnel were considered, but it was not until May 1959 that the first car drove over the new bridge. The Auckland Harbour Bridge, to give it its official name, is about 1,100 yards long and has to be high enough for ocean-going ships to pass safely under it at all states of the tide, so the roadway is about 140 feet above the high-water level, and the bridge is now of course a major feature in the Auckland scenery. With hindsight, and as perhaps we all might have known, it proved unable to cope with the increase in the flow of traffic over the years, and in the late 80s Japanese contractors were employed to add two new lanes on each side of the existing structure. These have ever since been known as Nippon Clipons and the bridge now caries eight lanes of traffic. Even this was not the answer and in 1990 a moveable barrier was installed so that at peak hours more lanes can be allocated to the busier flow of traffic. It sounds all quite logical, but when we came to drive over it in a hire car on a later occasion, we did find it all a bit confusing. However, familiarity breeds contempt and on our first crossing our host had no such worries.

Devonport has an old-world charm and is now very much the haunt of tourists. Many of the houses are original Victorian single-storey buildings, mostly of wood and painted in attractive pastel colours. Most still have corrugated tin roofs, which we thought rather quaint, being used to slates or clay tiles back home. We associate corrugated roofs with country chapels and old workshops and allotment huts, and only rarely does one see a house in Britain with such a roof. We thought perhaps they were used as a less expensive option, but in fact they aren't cheap. A new tin roof will cost a pretty penny and Kiwis will often work hard keeping it nicely painted, and, when necessary, will search for that elusive leak and stop it with bolt, nut and washer. And don't think the occupants live in a sweat box when the sun is high overhead in summer. The roofs are well-insulated, keeping the house cool in summer and warm in winter, and surprisingly the patter of rain is not intrusive. Also we must remember that New Zealand is prone to earthquakes and one can imagine what would happen, even in a minor rumble, were the roofs tiled with slates. So there's a lot to be said for the tin roof which we in the Northern hemisphere dismiss as cheap and unfashionable. Even the Esplanade Hotel, a very grand Victorian building in its time, though now looking slightly seedy, is roofed in painted corrugated iron. Opposite this survivor from a more dignified age, the passenger ferry, the Kestrel, a well-loved and restored veteran, still decants tourists who have crossed the water from the Ferry Building. Against a background of modern featureless high rise buildings, which make up the main centre of Auckland, the Ferry Building stands out as a veritable architectural gem. A red-brick four-storeyed structure with a façade ornamented with contrasting stone columns and arches and surmounted by a clock tower, it is a relic of earlier times, when the harbour was the main gateway for grateful travellers who had spent weeks on the high seas on the voyage from the old country. Now it advertises itself as an elegant shopping centre specialising in the duty-free trade, but in former times it would have housed the local offices of the Ferry Companies which regularly used the port to take people and cargo to the remoter areas of the North Island.

From Stanley Point we had a panoramic view of Auckland, with the Harbour Bridge off to the right, the commercial harbour and the Ferry Building just opposite and away to our left the city's eastern suburbs including St Helier's Bay. Below us was the naval base, HMNZS Philomel, with the naval barracks, hospital and its jetties where three RNZN Leander class frigates and some patrol boats were tied up. Until 1895 the people of New Zealand made no contribution to the colony's naval defence, but from then until 1913 made an increasing financial contribution to its cost and also paid for the construction of a battle-cruiser for the Royal Navy. The battle-cruiser was appropriately named HMS New Zealand and she visited Auckland in 1913, when the New Zealand Division of the Royal Navy was inaugurated. The cruiser HMS Philomel, after which the present naval base is named, was converted into a training ship and was permanently based in Auckland to train members of the division to serve in RN ships. Barely two years later the fledgling New Zealand Division, forming part of the crew of the battle- cruiser New Zealand, took part in the battle of The Dogger Bank in the North Sea some sixty miles east off the English coast, when the British fleet under the command of Admiral Beatty put Admiral Hipper and his ships to flight. Later she also saw action in the Battle of Jutland. But it was not until after the end of the Second World War in 1945 that the Royal New Zealand Navy, as we know it today, was formed and able in its own right to give such valuable service with the United Nations forces in the Korean war.

Later, before we left Devonport we drove up the narrow winding road which leads to Mount Victoria, which stands head and shoulders above the little town. Here the RNZN built its harbour signal station among the remnants of the fortifications, still visible to this day, of the Kawerau tribe. On our return to sea level we drove along King Edward's Parade, where at the end in Torpedo Bay stands a memorial to commemorate the arrival of the Maori canoe Tainui after its long voyage from that mythical place Hawaiki.

Devonport is full of interesting nooks and crannies, two museums and several craft shops, and we could and perhaps should have spent longer there, but as always time was limited and we had to leave.

If you visit the City of Sails you just have to get on the water and there are plenty of ferries and tourist boats to help you do just that, but they aren't quite right as they don't have sails! As a keen sailor, with a boat of my own, I was beginning to suffer from extreme withdrawal symptoms, when a kind friend observing my poor state of health, invited me for a sail.

The next day four of us set off in a handsome sloop-rigged yacht berthed in Westhaven, near the Nippon Clipon bridge, and ran before a fresh force five before turning to port to reach through the Rangitoto channel. We had a close up view of Rangitoto, with its beautiful conical outline followed by the heavily wooded Motutapu Island, joined by a causeway to its volcanic neighbour. Past Motutapu we altered course towards Waiheke Island, where we anchored for lunch in Onera Bay. From Auckland, Waiheke Island seems far off and I didn't expect to see so much habitation, but the beach was busy and in the hills around were pleasant houses, and though most were holiday homes, some were permanent housing. Homeward bound we beat against the wind passing on the other sides of Motutapu and Rangitoto and thence back to base. It was an exhilarating day and after sailing in the crowded waters of the Solent, the feeling of space was wonderful. I felt I could now really claim to have visited the City of Sails.

The time we had allowed for our wanderings in Auckland was fast running out, but before escaping for our wider travels, we were taken to the western shore of the Firth of Thames overlooking the Coromandel Peninsula to visit the Miranda bird sanctuary. The water here is shallow and at low tide many square miles of rich mud are exposed, attracting thousands of migratory birds. Keen but not expert bird-watchers, we were thrilled to see oyster-catchers by the hundred filling the air with their shrill penetrating calls as they flew with a marked sense of purpose from one productive expanse of mud to another. Caspian terns were also about with their black hats, stout red bills and black legs. Elegant stilts with fragile pink legs were easy to distinguish, but the sanderlings and their dumpier smaller cousins the knots were more difficult to see against the muddy foreshore. But the birds which we shall always remember were the bar-tailed godwits, which migrate from here to Siberia! It made us feel very humble when we thought how we had travelled from UK in the security, warmth and comfort of a Boeing 747!

Chapter Three

LAKE TAUPO

We left Auckland heading south on Highway 1, the road to Wellington, a fine dual carriageway full of commuter traffic. Just on the outskirts is Manuku City. This, said to be the fastest-growing urban development in New Zealand, was established in 1965 and after only 15 years had a population of about 200,000. It epitomises modern, affluent New Zealand and dare I say it, would easily be at home in any sunny, seaside location in almost any country. Its motto is "Ante Alios Prosili" – Be Ahead of the Times – which I think sums it up well. The city is twinned with Utsunomiya in Japan, which emphasises the importance New Zealand now attaches to its links with Japan. Indeed the countries of the Co-Prosperity Sphere that Japan wished to create in the Second World War, which nowadays are known as the countries of the Pacific Rim, now form New Zealand's major export market. Japanese tourists are everywhere and if there is a second language it's Japanese. On our flight out I noticed that Air New Zealand's In Flight magazine had a large section printed in Japanese, so it's quite clear that Japan is now a very important trading partner for the Kiwis.

As we drove along, I was studying the map and was delighted to see that we had safely passed Bombay, with its Collision Crossroads, without even noticing them! I wondered how this tiny village had acquired this oriental name. Had some retired Indian Army Colonel made this his final home, or had some Indian labourers been quartered here whilst building the highway?

We were now out in open country, with rolling pastures and grass-covered hills, and we began to see large stainless steel road tankers, some even towing trailers. Their cargo is not petrol, but milk collected from the dairy farms and taken to factories for processing into butter, cheese, dried milk and other dairy products. We passed one of these factories, a tall, gleaming building at a little place called Te Rapa just before Hamilton.

Huntly, with its coal-mines and coal-fired power station, sat astride our route, but like its UK counterparts it too is in decline and the power station is only maintained as a reserve source of electricity. Much of the country's power supplies are now met by hydroelectric schemes. The Waikato river, the longest river in the country, which starts in Lake Taupo and makes its way northwards through a number of dams and lakes, is the main source in this region. After driving through Hamilton, with the railway line running down the centre of the main street and then on to Cambridge, we stopped for a picnic on Lake Karipiro, which is one of the many lakes fed by the Waikato, and sure enough here was a dam and a power station. With its wooded shores the lake made an attractive setting for lunch and we enjoyed watching the sailing boats and water skiers and we learnt that its length and tranquillity make it ideal for water sports; and that both the 1950 Empire Games and the 1978 World Rowing Championships were held here.

On our journey south the Waikato kept us company, sometimes hiding behind the hills and sometimes disguising itself as Lake Arapuni or Lakes Maraetai, Whakamaru, Attamuri and Ohakuri until at last not far from our goal we parted company. What tongue-twisters we found these Maori names! But they are not so difficult when you realise that all syllables have equal importance and none is stressed at the expense of the others. If you pronounce TAKEAWAY as TA AK EY A A WAY you'll get the idea! But remember 'wh' sounds like an 'f', so 'Whaka' becomes 'Faka'.

As we said a temporary farewell to the Waikato we approached the Wairakei Geothermal Steam Power Project, whose presence is announced by great wisps of steam that drift alarmingly across the road. Here great numbers of boreholes have been driven several thousand feet into the earth to tap huge underground reservoirs of super-heated steam. This is then piped into turbo-generators to produce yet more electricity for the national grid. There is an interesting by-product at Wairakei, where an enterprising firm exploits the warm waters discharged from the turbines to grow a species of freshwater prawns, which normally only flourish in a tropical environment. Malaysian king prawns are used for breeding and the progeny are grown in four large tanks. The company gives guided tours to visitors. The largest prawn ever produced was about three feet long, but we settled for some which were about five inches in length, and paid fifteen dollars for a dozen, about forty pence each. They were delicious.

Just before we reached the town of Taupo we stopped to see the Huka Falls. Here the Waikato drops spectacularly through a narrow chasm into a deep pool beneath producing a very dangerous undertow, before wending its way northwards. 'Huka' means 'foam' and there is plenty about, but it is the solid opacity of the water which impresses. Legend has it that two Maori tribes who had a quarrel agreed to race down the river to settle the argument. The home team let the others draw ahead and stopped in time as their opponents were washed over the falls and drowned. A drastic but nevertheless effective solution to the problem!

Taupo stands at the north-eastern end of the lake, where the crystal clear waters of our friendly Waikato river fed by vast snow fields and glaciers leave for their long journey into the Tasman sea. Taupo is a huge lake of about 230 square miles and is some 1,000 feet above sea level, so it gives the river a vast amount of energy for conversion into electricity. The lake is the result of a massive volcanic eruption thousands of years ago, which diverted the mouth of the Waikato river from the Firth of Thames to its present estuary on the west coast. The waters rise on Mount Ruapehu forming the river Tongariro which enters the lake at Turangi at its southern end and leaves at Taupo township, where it becomes the Waikato river.

The lake is a centre for a vast number of water sports and activities, but fishing is the most popular. The shape of the lake is similar to the outline of the African continent and is overlooked on its western shores by mountains of the Hauhungaroa range. We continued through the town and drove along its eastern shore and just before Turangi we turned off and there on the edge of the lake at Stump Bay was our friends' bungalow. Some years earlier they had bought a "section" of about a quarter of an acre with an area of common land, known as Public Domain, in front giving it an uninterrupted view of the lake. Immediately to our left was the delta of the Tongariro river and opposite the Karangahape cliffs dropped sheer into the lake, while in the distance to our right the white pumice cliffs of Whangamata Bluffs reminded us of the cliffs at Dover. The bottom of the lake and the shore is sandy with a liberal sprinkling of pumice stones. When dry these are incredibly light and float on the surface, but they gradually soak up the water and sink. The pumice is also very soft and easily shaped, as I found when I tried to use it as a sanding agent on a piece of drift wood. The wood remained unchanged, while the pumice took up the shape of the wood!

The bungalow, which the Kiwis call a 'batch', was a wooden structure, with two good bedrooms and the usual offices and a splendid terrace on which to sit and enjoy the glorious view. We were therefore surprised to hear that it had been built off-site and delivered in one piece by road. But apparently this is quite usual, especially in Wellington, where I am told there are used house lots similar to used car lots, and one can wander around, in and out, selecting the house of one's choice, which will then be delivered to one's chosen site.

Lake Taupo is a Mecca for anglers and it is estimated that about 700 tons of trout are taken from the lake each year. The average weight is about four pounds, but seven and eight pounders are not uncommon. The approach to fishing for salmon and trout is quite different from that in the UK. New Zealand has a more egalitarian approach to all things and one does not obtain the right to fish for trout in a stream or lake here by the purchase of a rod. The fish belong to the state and the Kiwi angler buys a licence, which allows him to fish within a certain prescribed area.

The trout is not a native fish. In 1884 a shipment of brown and rainbow trout was liberated into the lake and its surrounding streams and rivers and all the trout in the area are descended from that one shipment. In 1923 a trout hatchery was established near Turangi on the banks of the fast-flowing Tongariro where it enters the lake. Here in the stripping pens the best male and female trout are milked for their milt and spawn and the two are mixed together producing tiny fish known as fry. One of the tanks we looked into held about 10,000 of these tiny fish only about two weeks old. They moved in one massive swirl whenever there was a possibility of food. Other tanks had older fish and outside in a large pond we saw the yearlings, again a swirling mass, but this time the fish were about nine to ten inches long and soon to be released into the rivers and streams. The hatchery has an observation room, the window of which looks into the stream at fisheye level. From here we could see the trout gently stemming the flow of the stream and admire the ease of its movements and the beauty of its form.

We walked through the grounds and along the river and saw several tuis. These are rather larger than a blackbird and have the slender curved beak of the honeyeater family. Their overall colour is black, though they have a greenish tinge and have a lacy white collar on the back and sides of the neck, with two prominent white appendages at the throat. These have earned them the name of 'parson bird'. Moving in and out of the reeds and vegetation at the water's edge were several pukekos, a member of the rail family and a native of New Zealand. They have a black head and upper parts with purplish-blue neck and breast with large red beaks and long slender red legs. Because of their habitat they are also called old swampies! We also saw black swans, natives of Australia but now resident here, and some New Zealand brown teal.

We accompanied our host, a keen angler, on a fishing expedition to Lake Kuratau but unfortunately he had no luck. We enjoyed the peace and solitude and tried our birdwatching skills. We saw both male and female paradise duck, a member of the shelduck family, with which we are familiar back home. Pied stilts with their white bodies and black wings were flying around with their long delicate pink legs trailing out behind, and we also saw herons and wrybills. The wrybill is a small grey-and-white plover, with a very unique feature in that the tip of the bill turns to the right, hence its name.

The approaches to the lake had been planted with pinus radiata, a conifer grown for wood pulp and newsprint, one of the many successful new industries being developed. On the lakeside we saw masses of hebe, broom, lupins and toetoe. Toetoe is a tall tussocky grass with long drooping leaves and taller stems with plume-like creamy seed-heads, which wave gracefully in the wind. The plant is also called 'cutty grass' because the edges of the leaves are razor-sharp. We also saw flax growing wild, long gladioli like spears some five or six feet long with groups of red tubular flowers, which mature into long black seed pods. For the Maoris, and later the Europeans, this has always been an important plant, because its tough leaves could be put to many uses. The cleaned fibre was used for making rope and cordage and along with timber has been one of the country's oldest exports. The Maoris also used it for weaving into clothing, mats and baskets, and even today it is used in making floor coverings.

Many of the smaller hills in the vicinity are still covered with what the locals call "native bush", among which we could distinguish the cabbage tree and the ponga fern. The cabbage tree looks like a small palm but with several heads. Its main trunk generally does not exceed three or four feet in height before it branches and it seems to be almost indestructible. Captain Cook made his crew eat the leaves, which are reputed to taste like cabbage, as fresh vegetables in order to ward off scurvy. Unlike the leaves, its wood is spongy and of no practical use. The ponga fern has fern-like fronds, which are silvery-white underneath. The trunk can be up to about 25 feet long and was split lengthways by the Maoris and driven into the ground to protect their fortified villages, and in fact it is still used for fencing, when the split logs often take root. Some of the larger trees we saw were rimu and kahikatea. The rimu is a member of the cupressus family and is also known as red pine, and is harvested for its good quality softwood. In 1769 Captain Cook reported seeing lofty trees, now known to have been kahikatea. He measured one and recorded that its girth at six feet from the ground was nineteen feet eight inches and the trunk, "straight as an arrow", measured 89 feet from the ground to the first branch. The kahikatea is also called the white pine because of its pale soft wood, which being odourless and light in weight was long used to make boxes in which butter in fifty-six pound slabs was packed for export.

Like all visitors to New Zealand we were always hopeful of sighting the national emblem, the kiwi. But kiwis are very rarely seen as they are nocturnal by habit. They are believed to be short sighted, but have a very strong sense of smell. They use their long bill to root out insect larvae and worms, though they also eat fallen fruits and insects on the surface of the forest floor.

The only non-domestic mammals we saw were possums, but sadly we saw them as road casualties. These grey furry animals with bushy tails, pointed snouts and long erect ears are also nocturnal and are frequently hit by passing cars and lorries; their maimed bodies are unhappy and frequent sights by the side of the road. The possum is not a native animal, but was introduced to establish a fur trade in 1858 and is now widespread in both the North and the South Islands. Like squirrels they spend most of their time in the trees, using their tail as an additional grip on branches as they move around, but they have an unexpected similarity to kangaroos. The female possum rears her young in a pouch.

Nearing home we stopped at the delta of the Tongariro in the hope of seeing some more bird life, which of course we did, but we were not rewarded with any fresh sightings. Nearby is Waihi, a Maori village situated on the lakeside, which we wanted to see, but our luck ran out. On the side of the road was a notice saying 'Private Locals Only'. We saw a local Maori at the door of his hut and asked whether we could go through to see the village, but he gruffly said no. So Waihi eluded us. I have since read about Waihi, which has been described as a magical little Maori village with a tiny upright church adorned with Maori art and motifs as well as the traditional symbols of the Roman Catholic faith, and close by is a burial ground containing the graves of Maori chieftains.

So our visit to Lake Taupo ended on a sad note with enmity still existing in places between Maori and Pakeha, but for all that the lake is a wonderful place. We left feeling that we had seen only one of its many faces and that we would like to renew our acquaintance with it when other seasons of the year give it a different aspect and character.

Chapter Four

TUKINO'S GIFT

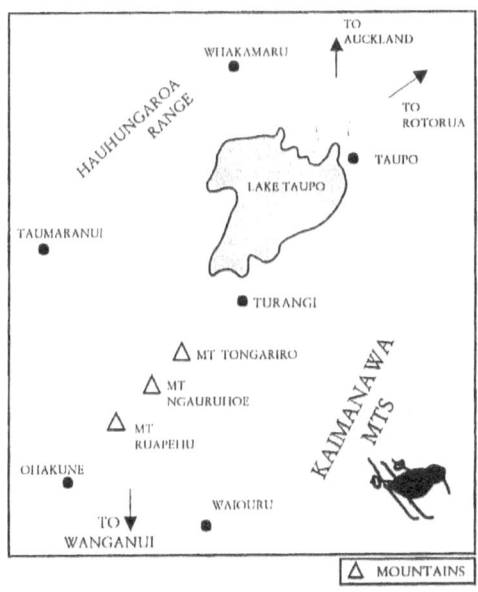

TONGARIRO NATIONAL PARK

To the south of Lake Taupo and dominating the skyline is the Tongariro National Park, which stands almost in the centre of the North Island and covers a huge area of some 171,000 acres. Its unforgettable features are the three volcanic peaks, which rise almost in a straight line from north to south. Formed over three million years ago, they are the southernmost link in a volcanic chain that stretches around the perimeter of the Pacific Ocean. Mount Ruapehu (9,175 ft), the southernmost and tallest of the three, is the highest mountain in the North Island and is over twice as high as Ben Nevis (4,406ft), the highest in UK. Still active from time to time, Ruapehu's summit is snow clad all year. In an act surely meant to remind mere mortals of his great macho virility, this sleeping giant erupted with awesome force in 1996 and reclaimed his sovereignty over his slopes as man and beast f led to safety. It was his most spectacular eruption in living memory. Mount Ngauruhoe, the next highest at 7,515ft, is the most active of the three and with its almost symmetrical cone, and the puffs of steam emanating from its crater is a truly splendid sight. The most northerly and also the smallest at 6,345ft is Mount Tongariro. Though it has several craters, it is the quietest of them all. The park owes its existence to a Maori chief, Te Heuheu Tukino, who gave the summits of the three mountains to the government in 1887 to avoid what he thought was the inevitable sale of the land to the Europeans. "They shall be", he said, "a sacred place of the Crown and a gift forever from me and my people".

In winter the slopes are heavily covered with snow and the park is the North Island's most popular ski resort. We climbed the road to the Whakapapa ski field on the side of Ruapehu. In the midst of summer this presented a desolate sight, with a jumble of black lava rocks covering the slopes among the chair lifts, chalets, car parks and all the paraphernalia of a ski resort. The snow just has to be deep to ski over that lot! At this altitude the air had a cold bite to it and although we tarried to take in the view as lava gave way to heather and tussock grass, with here and there the splash of yellow broom, we were grateful for the warmth which met us as we descended to lower levels.

It was now time for lunch, so we tramped a few hundred yards off the road in search of a picnic place. Our path swung to the left and there was the ideal spot. A small stream cascaded over a drop of about ten feet onto a rocky shelf, before f lowing over this into a deep rock pool, which drained into a larger stream. The whole area was covered in heather and grasses with clusters of broom and hebe here and there. We settled down to enjoy our cool beers and the superb view of the volcanoes above us. Just as we started on our sandwiches a very nice young man came round the corner, hesitated and then asked if we would mind him bringing his children along. Why shouldn't we share this lovely spot with a family, we thought. "Of course not," we replied and shortly afterwards along came two ten-year-olds, followed by two or three more until we had a school party of about twenty children and three teachers sharing our find. But what fun they had as they stripped down to their bathers and jumped and splashed and dived into the pool. And what fun we had watching them too!

Refreshed by our lunch and water show we continued south on Highway 1 and met the Rangipo Desert. To me the word desert conjures up a picture of immense wastes covered with golden sand sculptured into hills, ridges and mountains by the prevailing wind. The Sahara desert leaps to mind, but the Rangipo Desert lives up to the definition in my dictionary, namely an uninhabited, barren tract of land. After the productive farmland and dense areas of bush through which we had driven on our journey from Turangi, the change in the scenery came as a shock. I'm told that the prevailing westerly winds lose their moisture on the west facing slopes of the mountains and then sweep down on this arid land helping to create this inhospitable desert of grit and gravel. The desert is not much good to man nor beast, except the New Zealand Army, which uses this area as a training ground. Before the 1914–18 war Lord Kitchener visited New Zealand, no doubt on one of his Imperial inspection tours, and selected the Rangipo Desert as a good area for army training and exercises, and it has remained so ever since, as the Army Barracks and married quarters we passed at Waiouru confirmed.

In the midst of the Army cantonment, surrounded by World War II howitzers and tanks, is the Queen Elizabeth II Army Memorial Museum. Museums fascinate me and as I am an ex-serviceman military museums have a special pull. The exhibits in this museum reflect the past glory of the New Zealand Army and its forbear, the Armed Constabulary, and also tells the story of New Zealand as a colony and later a Dominion and its loyalty to, and sacrifice for, the British Crown.

When the Archduke Francis Ferdinand, heir to the Hapsburg throne, was assassinated in Sarajevo on 28th June 1914, it precipitated an immediate declaration of war by Austria-Hungary against Serbia. Like the sudden collapse of a house of cards, Europe became embroiled in war as four days later Germany declared war on Russia and on 3rd August was also at war with France. When Germany invaded Belgium a day later, Britain too became involved and declared war on Germany on 4th August 1914. None of these dramatic events threatened the existence or lifestyle of New Zealand, who like the United States of America could have kept clear of this madness which had overtaken Europe. Yet in concert with the other member nations of the Commonwealth, New Zealand, who only as recently as 1907 had become a Dominion, immediately declared war on Germany in support of Great Britain. Thus for the first time, from her remoteness in the South Pacific she became involved in international commitments. About a tenth of the population served in the New Zealand armed forces and over 100,000 of them served overseas. Many endured the awful conditions in the trenches in France and fell in the bloody battles of the Somme, Ypres and Passchendaele. Others served and died with the ANZAC forces during the disastrous campaign at Gallipoli in 1915. When the armistice was signed in that railway carriage at Compiègne on 11th November 1918 and the fighting subsided, the appalling cost of fighting for the Empire finally came home to this small nation of a million people. Nearly 17,000 men, one in sixty of the population, had been killed.

But the war to end wars only retarded the desires of the Germans to dominate Europe once more. These ambitions began to be articulated again by the new Chancellor, Adolf Hitler, who seized power after Field Marshal Paul von Hindenberg retired as President in 1933.

Hitler's ambitions to create a greater Germany were largely fulfilled by the annexation of Austria in 1938 and the Czechoslovakian provinces of Bohemia and Moravia the following year, but his desire for lebensraum in the east plunged Europe into war again when his troops marched into Poland on 1st September 1939. Two days later on 3rd September, the British Prime Minister, Neville Chamberlain, in concert with the French, issued an ultimatum to Germany to withdraw from Poland. Hitler ignored this and after a meagre twenty-one years of peace, the old protagonists were again at war.

Once more New Zealand, like the other Dominions, rallied to the aid of Great Britain and despatched troops for this distant war. By 1942 nearly a third of the male labour force was committed to the conflict as members of the armed services. The Kiwis fought with distinction throughout the war, mainly in the European sector. To name but a few of their main achievements, their airmen fought in the Battle of Britain and in most of the air battles with Germany. Their sailors in the cruiser Achilles together with their British compatriots in the cruisers Ajax and Exeter successfully hunted the German Pocket Battleship Graf Spee and the joint force, despite being outgunned, forced the German warship to take refuge in Montivideo harbour, where she was scuttled in December 1939. And their soldiers, who formed the New Zealand Division under the command of General Sir Bernard Freyberg, fought with distinction in Greece, Crete, the North African desert and in the campaign in Italy.

But in December 1941, a new dimension was added to the conflict, when without warning Japan attacked the US naval base at Pearl Harbour and crippled the US fleet. A few days later the Japanese, who were preparing to land in northern Malaya, sank the two prestigious British battleships, Prince of Wales and Repulse, which had been despatched to intercept the invasion fleet. Within three months not only had Hong Kong been captured, but the supposedly impregnable base of Singapore, on which the defence of British interests in the Far East depended, had surrendered to the victorious Japanese army.

For Britain and her dominions this was the darkest period of the war and with the Dutch East Indies, now Indonesia, and the Philippines also in Japanese hands, New Zealand and Australia both found themselves in the front line with their troops on the other side of the world. In New Zealand a force of youngsters and veterans of the 1914–18 war was hastily mobilised, in similar fashion to the Home Guard in UK, and armed with ancient weapons prepared to defend their homeland. But by the middle of 1942, US forces began to arrive in the country and the defence was more certain as New Zealand became a training-ground for the long fight back up the island chain to the Japanese homeland.

When the war in Europe and the Pacific was finally over, the casualty rate in this second war was lower, but even so 11,600 Kiwis were killed. In this post-war period the consequences of the decline in British power in the Pacific and the rise of Japan's, together with New Zealand's new-found dependence on US protection, put a new perspective on the relations between New Zealand and Great Britain.

As the world shrinks and communities merge and new trading partnerships and defence relationships are formed, loyalties are bound to change; but to me it is still a wonderful thing that in two World Wars men and women from such a distant and remote land should volunteer, fight and die to help rescue Britain from the clutches, first of the Kaiser and then of Adolf Hitler.

The museum at Waiouru is most certainly worth a visit. Displays tell the stories of the early wars with the Maoris who felt their way of life threatened by the materialistic and land-hungry settlers. The army's involvement in the Boer War, showing memorabilia of the Boers and the New Zealand Mounted Riflemen who were sent to reinforce the British Army is remembered. Remembered too is the service rendered by the Pakeha and the Maoris together at Gallipoli and on the Western Front during the Great War of 1914–18 and also in North Africa, Crete and Italy during the Second World War. We must have spent an hour and a half there and I could have spent more, but we all have to, or at least should, abide by the edict of the majority vote and so off we went.

On our return to Lake Taupo we took the road which passes to the west of the three volcanoes and the countryside took on a different appearance as we left the desert behind. On our way south between Auckland and Hamilton we had passed through fields of onions ready for harvest. Now we found ourselves in one huge carrot farm, which centres itself on the township of Ohakune. We have bought New Zealand carrots in the UK during the winter, when the English variety have been exhausted, and at a quiz in our local gardening club we had been asked the weight of the world's biggest carrot. We all laughed when some brave soul said four pounds, but The Guinness Book of Records gives the answer. A carrot weighing 15 pounds 7 ounces was grown in Nelson, at the north end of the South Island, by a Mr Scott in 1978. But the record for the longest, at six feet ten and a half inches, grown in 1991, is held by Mr Bernard Lavery of Llanharry, Mid Glamorgan. We were reminded about our gardening club quiz when we saw this huge model carrot some 6 feet tall standing up on the verge outside the entrance to a carrot farm.

The road now ran alongside the Whakapapa river, which was soon joined by the Whanganui as we approached Taumarunui where we crossed the Auckland to Wellington railway line. This was the scene of New Zealand's greatest railway disaster, which cruelly occurred on Christmas Eve 1953. It must have been a terrifying spectacle as melting ice on the mountain above transformed the placid Whakapapa river into a roaring and rampaging monster carrying all before it, while from the south the Auckland express bearing passengers full of Christmas joy ran into its path. The bridge had been carried away and the train plunged to its destruction into the swollen river with the loss of one hundred and fifty-one lives. This tragedy occurred when the new Queen was visiting her faraway dominion and she was able to share the grief of her subjects at first hand. Many years later in 1989, the Lions and Lioness Clubs of towns in the vicinity, together with the New Zealand Railways and other companies, erected a monument on the site to remember this tragedy. The location of the old bridge was abandoned and a new one erected a little further downstream.

After a pause at this sombre spot we turned and headed back for the bungalow on Lake Taupo for a final swim in the cool clear water and a last evening with our friends, before we set off on the morrow on our own for the next leg of our travels.

Chapter Five

THE SECOND LAKE

ROTORUA

with much reluctance we left our hosts and their delightful bungalow, with its superb views over the lake and the mountains beyond, and made our way to Turangi, where we had arranged to collect our hire car. Our car was not available immediately as it had to be brought from the depot at Taupo some thirty miles away, but our delay made us realise there were other ways to get around. The railways, like their counterparts in other lands, have very rigid routes and most of the young if they can't hitchhike use the long-distance buses, which seemed in great demand. It seems important to book as one poor couple found out when the bus to Wellington came to a halt alongside the booking office, which seemed to double as the car hire office as well. Not only had they not booked, but in addition to the inevitable back packs, they had bicycles as well! So they had a difficult task not only negotiating two seats for themselves but even more so, space on the roof rack for their bikes. At first it looked improbable, but the lady in charge of the booking office showed great patience and spent a long time on the phone and eventually with a smile she announced that all was well and loading commenced.

This little interlude kept us amused while we waited for our car, which arrived shortly after the bus left. We completed the formalities and before setting off I enquired whether there were any restrictions on the use of the car. Could we for instance drive on unsealed roads? "Yes of course," we were told, but on no account were we to drive on 90 Mile Beach right up on the north west coast. With that exception we could drive wherever it was reasonable to do so.

With those perimeters firmly in mind we set off driving on the left hand side of the road, with very similar rules to those which apply back home.

We retraced our route past the lake to Taupo, past the Huka Falls and the clouds of steam which heralded the approach of the boreholes at Wairakei, and shortly afterwards we left Highway 1 and branched off onto the road to Rotorua. Our route took us through meadows and pastures grazed largely by cattle, but here and there horses, before the road entered the Tahorakuri Forest. This is the smallest of three huge man-made forests of pine trees in this area. The trees grown are mainly radiata pines, also known as the monterey pine, which are grown for lumber and pulp. These are natives of California and have beautiful long straight trunks with branches covered in dark green needles in groups of three. They make a very dense woodland and eventually grow to a height of 110 to 120 feet. But here they are harvested after 25 years, when they will be about 65 to 70 feet tall, and an ongoing replanting programme ensures a continual supply.

New Zealand

We left the forest and crossed our old friend the Waikato River and shortly afterwards the scenery changed once more. From pleasant pasture it changed to a land of little hummock-like rounded hills, up which sheep, cattle and even deer grazed their way. With mountains in the distance and a smell of sulphur pervading the air, we knew we were fast approaching our destination.

The smell of sulphur, or strictly speaking hydrogen sulphide, is constant, and is part of the way of life in the city which has been referred to as Sulphur City. I suppose the locals get used to the smell and probably don't even notice it, but with us it was a constant, if unwelcome companion! Rotorua is a popular spa resort and visitors still seek the curative powers of the hot thermal pools, and the Polynesian Pools in the centre of town are, I suppose, the place to visit for an authentic thermal bath. But many hotels and private homes have their own pool, as indeed did the motel we chose for our stay, though I must confess we didn't use it.

Rotorua in fact sits on a huge underground lake of hot water and steam, and here and there one sees steam seeping up through gutters, bushes and even flower beds. The locals even sink bores in their gardens and harness the steam to heat their homes and swimming-pools.

On its northern edge sits Lake Rotorua, a sizeable lake of some 23,000 acres. It is a Maori name and Rotorua merely means 'second lake'. What a sad translation! A smaller lake to its east is called Lake Rotoiti, which means first. It is said that when the Maori canoe, the Arawa, made land just to the north on the shores of the Bay of Plenty, the exploring party discovered a large lake which they named "first lake" and later a second bigger one which they named "second lake". Had they by chance travelled by a different route the famous Sulphur City might now be known as Rotoiti!

As we sat on the edge of Lake Rotorua, enjoying the peaceful setting with its backdrop of mountains, I mused at the wonder of this great Maori immigration. If Hawaiki, their traditional homeland is in fact in the Marquesas Islands, it was indeed a wonderful achievement. They had no compass to steer by, nor any charts to enable them to lay off a course, and the distance travelled must have been at least two to three thousand miles. Polynesian seamen are renowned for their apparent ability to navigate over huge distances and I believe often use bird life as indicators, and also the clouds which frequently form over islands in the Pacific. Perhaps the very name they gave to New Zealand, 'Aotearoa', meaning 'The Land of the Long White Cloud' suggests that steering by selected clouds was one of the navigators' secrets. And what shape did the canoes take? A dugout canoe is not very stable and surely is an unlikely vessel on which to venture too far from land. I believe it is now generally accepted that the vessels were double canoes joined together by booms over which some form of decking was fastened, making what we now call a catamaran, the Tamil name for a double-hulled boat. On the decking some sort of shelter was probably erected using palm fronds or other such material. In addition to paddles, they probably had a lateen type sail set from a single mast. We cannot know for certain, but Tasman, when he sighted the west coast of the South Island in the mid seventeenth century, certainly reported seeing "double canoes", which was probably an accurate report, as they were the ones which attacked his boat and inflicted casualties.

I wondered whether some intrepid Maoris might one day endeavour to trace the mythical route of their ancestors in a reconstructed canoe, using the South East trade winds and the South Equatorial and East Australian currents to retrace their voyage from the Marquesas Islands.

As I awakened from my reverie my eyes strayed upon Mokoia Island in the centre of the lake and I recalled reading a Maori love story. It concerned a young Maori maiden, called Hinemoa, who lived on the shores of Lake Rotorua. She fell in love with a young chief, Tutanekai, who belonged to an opposing tribe and lived on Mokoia Island. To go to him she planned to sail across the waters in a canoe, but unable to elude members of her own tribe, she couldn't reach the island. Maddened by her failure and bewitched by the sounds of Tutanekai playing his flute, she slipped into the water under cover of darkness and swam, landing on the island at Hinemoa's pool. The young chief's slave, having been sent to get some cool water for his master, found the maiden, who asked him for a drink of water. Having drunk she smashed the cup, whereupon the slave returned to his master to report the insult. Tutanekai seized his club and rushed to challenge the stranger, only to find his beloved. He placed his cloak around her and led her to his hut and they were married and lived happily ever after. Surely this is a love story which is the stuff of opera, with moving arias and all the drama which goes with this great art form!

Rotorua is perhaps New Zealand's prime tourist attraction and is famous for its thermal activity. The first thermal pool we visited was at Tikitere, south of Lake Rotoiti, and is called Hell's Gate after the largest boiling whirlpool in the area. The temperature of the water in the pool is reported to be ninety eight degrees centigrade and the depth of the pool has not been ascertained. With a higher than usual concentration of sulphur in our nostrils we made our way around some 20-odd pools, obeying the warnings not to stray from the paths as in places the ground is unstable. How difficult it is to comply with these instructions, when with a camera slung round one's neck one sees that beautiful and rare bird perched on some twig over there! Some tourists have been burnt and scalded and some have in fact died, so beware. The mud pools were fascinating as hot mud plops up from the depths forming weird sculptures and at the Kakahi Falls, where the temperature of the water is about forty degrees centigrade, the public used to take hot showers for their health. Hottest is the Inferno, where the water temperature is reported to reach one hundred and eleven degrees centigrade at times. How can water be hotter than one hundred degrees centigrade I asked? Apparently the graphite in suspension is the reason and it is this that gives the water its eerie gunmetal colour.

The Whakarewarewa Thermal Reserve on the southern edge of the city should not be missed if only for the geysers. The biggest is Pohutu Geyser, said to send plumes of steam and water up to about a hundred feet, though on the day we went there it seemed to be very wheezy and definitely out of sorts. Perhaps geysers can suffer from asthma too! There are in fact two entrances to the Reserve, but the more impressive takes you through an ornately carved gateway straddling thick palisades which defend the replica of a fortified Maori village, a Pa no less. The two figures at the gateway represent the two lovers of the lake, Hinemoa and Tutanekai. Within the village is the Maori Arts and Craft

Institute, which was formed with government assistance in the 1970s to help keep alive Maori art and culture. Much of their art is portrayed in strange, powerful and, to my mind, threatening carvings, and the Institute trains young Maori carvers in the art over a three year period. Maori ethics do not allow women to carve, but they demonstrate the traditional weaving of flax and basket and mat making.

We had booked into a motel on the long tree-lined boulevard which takes the visitor into the centre and we returned thither in need of rest and relaxation. Though utilitarian, our accommodation was comfortable and like most motel rooms in the country had a well appointed kitchen with sink, cooker and fridge. Clearly in New Zealand tourists expect to cook for themselves, but we were weary and found a convenient takeaway close by.

In the 1850s and '60s one of the great tourist excursions in the country started from a little Maori village called Te Wairoa, not far from Rotorua. Visitors were taken by boat and canoe across Lakes Tarawera and Rotomahana to gaze at the famous Pink and White Terraces on the sides of Mount Tarawera which overshadows the lakes. These terraces were natural 'staircases' formed by thermal action spreading coloured deposits of silica over rocks in delicate pink and white. They looked so spectacular that at the time many New Zealanders claimed they were the eighth wonder of the world.

The village had a hotel for visitors, a water-powered wheat mill, a blacksmith's shop, a meeting house and many huts for the locals. On the surrounding slopes stretched fruit orchards, wheatfields and other cultivated areas. All this was to be destroyed on 10th June 1886, when Mount Tarawera erupted with explosive force at one thirty a.m. blasting thousands of tons of molten rock and boiling mud into the night sky. Not only did the famous terraces disappear, but enormous quantities of ash, lava and mud were deposited on the surrounding area and much of this was thrown down on to the village.

In the chaos and confusion people dashed from their houses to find safe shelter. As molten ash and mud rained down, they ran to the nearest refuge and for many this was the Maori Meeting House, which had been named Hinemihi. The building's steeply sloping roof allowed the hot wet mud to slide down on to the ground around it. Those sheltering inside picked up the long benches lining the walls and used them to prop up the sagging roof, which threatened to cave in as the ground shook and more mud arrived.

Dozens sheltered inside the Meeting House and all were saved. Outside one hundred and fifty-three people perished, including over one hundred Maoris. So great was the eruption that 3,000 square miles of land was affected by mud and dust deposits. The sound of the eruption was heard in Wellington some 290 miles to the south and the glare from the volcano was seen clearly in Wanganui 190 miles away.

When daylight came to Te Wairoa, rescuers found that where once stood the 'eighth wonder of the world', there was now a gigantic basin throwing red hot mud and rocks into the clouds of steam above. Everything in sight was covered in mud and lava and every building had been smashed and buried under eight feet of ash. All that is except for one, the Meeting House, Hinemihi.

The village, which has now rightly acquired the name 'The Buried Village', has been partly excavated and portions of the hotel and other buildings are now uncovered and there is an interesting collection of relics, which are on display in the museum. The Tohunga's whare, the priest's house, can also be seen. The priest, who was reputed to be one hundred and ten years old, did not predict the coming disaster and was blamed for it by the tribe. At first the survivors would not allow him to be rescued from his buried house, but after four days they relented. Incredibly, when they did dig him out he was still alive, but he died a few days later.

The remains of the village is now a tourist attraction and there are pleasant paths along which to amble and reflect on this fearful night. There is also a signposted walk along the Te Wairoa stream, which powered the mill, but this is not for the faint-hearted. The early part is gentle as one strolls along the side of the stream, where one can see the bow section of one of the canoes used on the lakes. But then it becomes rather like an obstacle course as one descends by a track, then through the bush and finally by ladder through a cave. Throughout one has dramatic views of the stream as it cascades in two falls over about 300 feet and the walk and the subsequent climb back is well worth it.

On our way home, we stopped and looked across the lake at the culprit, Mount Tarawera, now quiet and serene, but reminding us of Table Mountain with the long flat ridge on its top marking the crater which was formed when that mass of rock, lava and debris was hurled into the night a century ago.

Some time later, when we were back in England we visited Clandon Park, the home of the Earl of Onslow, which is not far from Guildford. Having toured the house we walked around the gardens and there, lo and behold, was a Maori Meeting House and none other in fact than Hinemihi! The fourth Earl was Governor-General of New Zealand at the time of Mount Tarawera's eruption and three years later was searching for some permanent reminder of New Zealand to take home to Clandon Park. After four terms as Governor-General he had come to love the country and had even given his infant son a Maori name, Huia, in honour and respect for the country and its people. The Earl saw the remains of the Meeting House and bought the building outright for £50 and arranged for it to be transported back to England, where it was erected in the grounds of his home. In the 1970s the English National Trust, into whose possession Clandon Park was given, decided that Hinemihi was in need of repair and with guidance from the Rotorua Art Gallery it was restored to its former glory.

Having left the Buried Village we felt in need of a more cheering spectacle to give us back our holiday spirit. We had heard of the Agrodome and its live sheep show and shearing display and decided to pay it a visit. The complex is on beautiful farmland to the west of Lake Rotorua with Mount Ngongotaha, about two-thirds as high as Mount Tarawera, to its west. It is a family business founded in 1970 by George Harford and Godfrey Bowen and it has flourished ever since, though their sons now run the 300 acre farm and the shows.

The main show takes place in a purpose built theatre, with a stage backed by a series of terraces. A very muscular and cheerful young farmer with a good Kiwi accent came on stage and said a few introductory words before calling one of the stars of the show to come and make an appearance. On came a huge ram with beautiful curly horns and a thick fleece. He climbed up the steps until he was at the top of the back terrace, whereupon he took a few titbits from a strategically placed feeding tray, while our friendly farmer told us he was a pedigree merino ram. Until then we did not know that this breed was indigenous to Spain, nor that it is mainly grown for its very fine wool and that it can be kept on the poorest and driest districts. A further eighteen stars, all pedigree rams, made their entrance one by one and climbed to their allotted place, while their characteristics were explained to us. Most were of British stock, such as the Dorset Horn, the Drysdale, the Hampshire and the Cheviot, but we did see the Texel, a breed from the Netherlands. All these pedigree rams had been bred on the farm and now run with the ewes, when in season, to prolong their breed.

We were also given a display of shearing and were shown how the animal is controlled by the way it is sat back on its haunches to keep it still. A full-grown ewe and especially the ram is a heavy beast, but our farmer handled them with ease, which explained his well-muscled frame. He told us that an average shearer using electric shears can shear about 300 animals in a day and that they get paid by the number of animals they cope with. If they have to shear by hand the number falls to about 200 and they get double pay. He completed shearing his ewe and lifted up the fleece for us to see that it had come away in the one piece. The average fleece weighs about eleven pounds and the sheep are shorn every eight months.

He told us that the ewes are kept until they are about six years old, when their teeth have been worn down by the pumice in the ground and they can then no longer feed properly. At that time they will have produced somewhere between five and seven lambs and about 80 pounds of wool. New Zealand is the third biggest producer of wool in the world with an annual production of some 360,000 tonnes, about half that of Australia, which has the highest output. The human population of New Zealand is a little over 3 million and the sheep population is 60 million, so there are almost twenty sheep for every human being!

We learnt that the Kiwis do not particularly like eating lamb, they prefer to eat the meat of an animal in its second year, when it is known as hogget and has a much better flavour. Unfortunately we never could find any hogget on the menu and lamented the sad loss of mutton from our British butchers. Where does all the mutton go these days? Ewes are still eventually slaughtered and I suppose nowadays they end up mainly as pet food, which is big business. What an indictment of our modern, affluent fast-food society, when even pets rarely if ever get anything to eat that doesn't come out of a tin!

The sheep dogs on the farm are not the traditional type we know in UK. Their dogs were very agile and obedient and barked a lot. They bark to frighten the sheep so that they can be herded and they are trained to run over the backs of the sheep to get to the other side of the flock in order to turn them. The traditional border Collies, which they also use, do not bark, but seem to stalk the sheep and fix them with their eyes and almost will them to do want is wanted. Both types of dog displayed their skills herding sheep and driving them into pens in the paddock outside.

The Agrodome is very well worth a visit; it was a most interesting and amusing show, which changed our mood after the Buried Village.

We drove back to our hotel through the town, which has many modern flat-roofed buildings, with here and there the odd high rise, too small to be called a skyscraper but nevertheless dominating its neighbours. The streets are laid out in a gridiron, making it easy to find one's way around, but the town itself really does not leave much of an impression once one has driven off. The only feature, other than the lake, which does stand out in this otherwise unmemorable town is the Government Gardens. These were created to enhance Rotorua's image as a spa resort and to emulate the elegance of European resorts. We turned off Hinemaru Street and drove down Queens Drive, where a huge statue of Queen Victoria stands at the end and just by our great Imperial Queen is the Bath House. This enormous timber-framed Tudor-style house, with red timbers and white infill, looks somewhat out of place in this subtropical setting amidst palm trees on the shores of the lake. But of course when it was built in the Victorian era, the settlers looked to the old homeland for its traditions and culture and the timber-framed Tudor style, which has so often been copied in other parts of the empire, such as Simla, Kuala Lumpur and Colombo, was clearly an obvious choice for British settlers in a land where timber was plentiful. Nowadays their thoughts are less focused on their British heritage, and more on their geographical position and their major trading partners. It was therefore understandable that the Union Jack was not among the six national f lags f lying in the breeze at their f lagstaffs in the gardens, where in addition to the New Zealand f lag f lew those of nations of the Pacific rim: the United States, Canada, Australia, Japan and Malaysia. The Bath House has since fallen victim to the corrosive forces of the thermal waters, which discolour water taps and fittings and metals. Some people even say that you can identify 'Rotorua money' by the dullness of the coins. The Bath House in fact no longer houses any thermal baths and has now been converted into a museum housing Maori carvings and arts. Those eager tourists wishing to take the cure are now directed to the modern building opposite called the Polynesian Pools.

On the lawns in front of this outrageously English building, the very English game of croquet was being played with much vigour by members of the local club. The players were all dressed in smart white shorts and dresses and all wore sun hats. With the sporadic thud of mallet against croquet ball and the click of ball against ball, one felt the years had been turned back to the days of empire.

Rotorua is one of the traditional homes of the Maori people and we had begun to learn a little about them during our brief visit and though time was short, we had one last visit to make to increase our growing knowledge of these early immigrants. On the shores of the lake not far from the Government Gardens lies Ohinemutu. Even today it is truly a Maori village in that the only inhabitants are Maoris, though today they no longer live in huts, but in European style houses.

One could be excused for calling it a hamlet, it is so small, but village it is as the presence of a church clearly confirms. St Faith's Church, an Anglican Church, which stands on the water's edge, towers above it and gives it its real identity. The first Christian service to be held in the Rotorua area was celebrated in this village on 30th October 1831, when the Reverend Henry Williams and Thomas Chapman visited the area. In 1835 a chapel was built but this was soon destroyed in inter-tribal warfare. Some fifty years later in 1885 the first real church was completed and in 1910 it was replaced by the existing building.

Like the Bath House in the Government Gardens, this too was built in the Tudor style and once again the colours are an unfamiliar red and white. As we entered we met the verger, who was a Maori. He was very proud of St Faith's and showed us around telling us that he liked the English as they always showed respect for the church. After such uninvited praise we felt we had better be on our best behaviour. He told us that the very first vicar was a Maori called Ihaia te Ahu who was in his mid-fifties. He had been trained by Thomas Chapman, who said of him: "He came to me in 1833 as a small boy and has been with me ever since; he has been a consistent Christian for the last forty years". The services were and still are conducted mainly in the Maori language. The interior of the church is rich in Maori carvings, with the tapestries decorated with Maori designs and made of flax twine dyed with traditional mud dye. Five figures at the base of the pulpit are demi-gods of Maori myth seen to be supporting the coming of Christianity.

In the mid-sixties the building was enlarged and a new choir-room, sacristy and chapel were added and the church was re-dedicated in 1967. The interior of the new chapel is in the form of a chief's house. The ceiling is decorated with black and white scrolls using a hammerhead shark pattern, which signifies dignity, prestige and agility, and the wooden panels on the walls are decorated with Maori motifs. But the most striking and unforgettable feature is the Galilee Window after which the chapel takes its name. A life-sized figure of Christ has been etched onto plate glass, which looks out over Lake Rotorua. It depicts Our Lord walking on the lake wearing a Maori chief's cloak adorned with Kiwi feathers and is very realistic and moving.

Outside we wandered through the graveyard which surrounds the building. Most graves remembered leaders of the tribe and other prominent Maoris, but among them is buried Edith Elizabeth Knaggs, who was the organist for many years. Just opposite the entrance porch is a statue of the great white Queen from over the seas. Queen Victoria presented this to all the loyal Maori tribes as a token of her gratitude for their support in the Maori wars.

As we left St Faith's we looked over our shoulder and saw Mokoia rising detached and aloof out of the lake and remembered the hostility of Hinemoa's tribe for the Arawa people, who lived on the island.

CHAPTER SIX

THE BAY OF ISLANDS

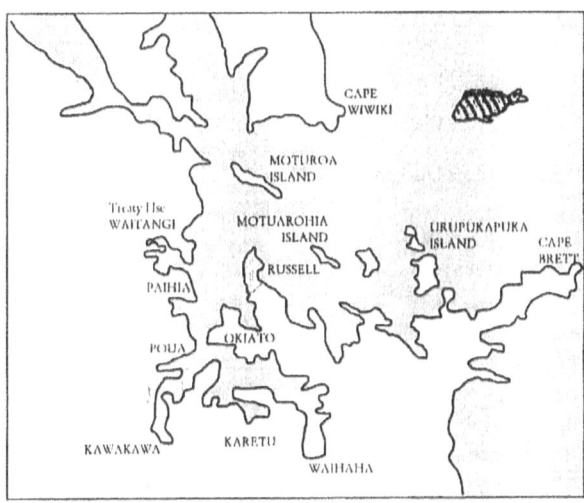

We left Rotorua on Highway 5 and soon we had purged our nostrils of that constant smell of sulphur and were once again enjoying the clean fresh air we had come to expect in this beautiful country. At Tirau we rejoined Highway 1 and retraced our steps through Hamilton and Manukau to Auckland. Once again we passed through Bombay without seeing anyone looking remotely like an Indian, but we could not be sure. Did we sniff the aroma of cumin and turmeric and coriander we wondered? Perhaps our sense of smell had been degraded by Sulphur City and these were just ordinary rural scents. We never knew as we sped northwards towards our next destination, the Bay of Islands.

We negotiated the Nippon Clipon and entered fresh territory as we left Auckland astern. Soon we could see the Whangaparaoa Peninsula jutting out into the Hauraki Gulf and before we knew it we were driving over the Weiti and Orewa rivers and entering Orewa, a pleasant seaside resort. We stopped for lunch and parked overlooking the beach and Whangaparaoa Bay. No crowds of sunburnt bathers on sunbeds or sheltering under sunshades in serried rows met our eyes on this lovely summer's day. This beach, about two miles long, was practically empty and we were able to share our lunch with red billed gulls and southern blackbacked gulls and watch the distant acrobatics of a tern as it dodged the attacks of a persistent skua.

Refreshed, we continued our journey, and for a short time after we had passed Waipu, the road ran along the shore of Bream Bay giving us lovely views of the sea and coastline, with the Hen and Chickens Group of islands off in the distance. Near these islands on 19th June 1940 the reality of the war against Nazi Germany was brought home to the locals when the Royal Mail ship Niagara struck a mine and sank in seventy fathoms (420 feet) of water. As she was loaded with bullion, this was a very serious loss and in December 1940 work began to salvage her valuable cargo. When twelve months later this had been completed ten tons of gold had been recovered. Quite a feat in such deep waters, but the effort was worthwhile as the gold was valued at the time at about two and a half million pounds!

Soon we were entering Whangarei, with its harbour protected by Bream Head to the east. Captain Cook and the crew of the Endeavour were the first Europeans to find this sheltered place, when they anchored here in November 1769. Like seamen the world over, they started fishing and Cook records in his log that they had soon caught nearly one hundred bream to supplement their meagre supplies. To remember this happy event Cook named the headland Bream Head. European settlement here started in 1839 but came to an abrupt halt six years later, when war with the local Maoris broke out. But after this hesitant start the region was exploited for its timber. Nowadays it is a busy port and a yacht marina and has a small airport. We had read about the nearby Whangarei Falls which are a tourist attraction. They are on the road north east of the city, which runs alongside the Ngunguru River, and can be seen from the bridge. The falls sounded worthwhile, but you can't always see everything and this was something we had to miss.

Just north of Otaika, we saw a vineyard with a sign saying Continental Wines. We had yet to buy some wine and drove up to the office, where we were met by a nice lady, who sounded Austrian. No, she was from Slovenia, part of the former Yugoslavia, but had emigrated many years ago. When they arrived she and her husband opened a drapery and general store in nearby Whangarei, which they ran for about twenty years. But in 1969 trade had started to fall off and they decided to use the knowledge the family had acquired in Slovenia and start a vineyard. Now, twenty-odd years later, it spreads over some twenty-five acres on the slopes of the hill behind their house. The vineyard is run by her husband who employs two men on a permanent basis and she and her daughter-in-law also help. We tried her Chardonnay, Pinot Noir and Cab Sav (as all Cabernet Sauvignon is called in New Zealand). The Müller-Thurgau, a white wine which she said was similar to her native Slovakian wines, pleased our palate and this is what we bought. On the counter she had a lovely large brass cash register, which must have been made some time in the 1920s. It still only registers pounds, shillings and pence, so she couldn't use it for its proper purpose. However, she still kept her money in it, and to open the drawer she had to ring up 'Change', when the bell gave a resounding clang and the drawer opened. I had visions of those lovely vacuum tubes we used to see in departmental stores, into which the sales assistant placed the money and bill in a little canister. Then she would pull a lever and with a hiss money, bill and canister would be sucked along to the cashier, who sat in the holy of holies recording the sale and dispensing the change. But the vineyard had no sophisticated system like that, just a lovely shiny brass cash register and a modern desk-top calculator to do the sums.

At Kawakawa we left Highway 1 and took the small road leading to Paihia, a beach resort on the Bay of Islands, where we found a hotel. The Bay of Islands is one of the country's top tourist attractions. Not only is it a lovely bay full of beautiful islands with tiny outcrops, sandy beaches and secluded coves and famous for its deep-sea fishing and wonderful diving opportunities, but it is also one of the country's most historic areas. In fact this is really the place to start a tour of New Zealand, as this is where the story of the colonisation of the land and the eventual acceptance by the tribes of Queen Victoria as their protector really starts.

When Captain Cook sailed Endeavour into the Bay of Islands in December 1769, after having discovered the new land a few months earlier, three Maori tribes had already established themselves in the area and a settlement had been formed at Kororareka, on the shores of the bay. Other explorers followed in Cook's wake. Two months after the Endeavour left, the Frenchman De Surville came to the Bay, and his brutal treatment of the natives led to the massacre of his countryman Marion du Fresne three years later. Spanish and Italian expeditions also followed and knowledge of this new land began to spread and adventurers pondered its potential for all sorts of new resources.

In the last decade of the eighteenth century a vessel from New South Wales left a gang of sealers at Dusky Sound on the south west coast of the South Island. They had such a rich harvest that soon small camps of sealers were being established at many places along the coast, and the indiscriminate slaughter of bulls, cows and pups began. At about the same time ships began hunting the sperm whale, which was abundant in these waters, and within a short time British, French and American whalers were regularly visiting these seas in search of whales. Another seafarer in search of profit brought the Fancy from Sydney to this new land and spent three months in the Hauraki Gulf collecting timber for spars. This proved a very successful enterprise and he was soon followed by other traders. Flax was another commodity sought by the foreigners. Thus a busy trade sprang up, chiefly with New South Wales, and in consequence the local tribes were drawn into the activities of the white men, the Pakehas as they came to call them, and many were used as labour to fell the massive trees and drag them down to the sea. The Maoris coveted the superior tools and weapons of the Pakehas and soon were trading sweet potatoes, flax and even their women for nails to fashion into fish hooks and even to flatten into simple chisels. Red cloth was torn into strips to be woven into cloaks, as red was their favourite colour, and their appetite for the Europeans' goods grew until they were also trading for liquor and muskets.

Ships also began anchoring in New Zealand waters and, emulating the British Navy's Press Gangs, started kidnapping the natives as crew for their ships. A prison chaplain encountered these dark-skinned men covered with strange tattoos on the wharves in Sydney. He wanted to know what land they came from and when he learnt more about them he determined to save them and their people from paganism and exploitation. Thus the rush to exploit the country's resources also brought missionaries to the land.

By now the many whalers operating in these waters were in need of a port where they could reprovision and carry out repairs. Kororareka, sheltered in the Bay of Islands, filled this need and gradually its European population grew: a mixture of deserting seamen, runaway convicts from Australia, grog sellers and those who provided for the sailors' most basic needs, as well as respectable traders. By the 1830s as many as one hundred and fifty ships were calling at the port each year and the victualling of these ships became a very profitable business. But as the number of ships calling for supplies grew, the township rapidly gained the reputation of a lawless and bawdy port and acquired the name of the "Hellhole of the Pacific". Here and in other parts of the country the Maoris had the opportunity to observe at close hand the ways of the Pakehas. Needless to say, since the people they met were generally of the most brutalised and degraded sort they grew to detest them. Visiting seamen infringed Maori laws and customs in innumerable ways. They defied their sacred taboos, stole their possessions to sell as curiosities and their crops for food; molested their women and kidnapped their men without scruple.

In 1815 the first mission station was set up by the Reverend Samuel Marsden and on Christmas Day the gospel was preached on New Zealand soil for the first time. His text came from the gospel of St Luke: "Behold I bring you good tidings of great joy". But the good tidings did not seem to interest the Maoris. After setting up his mission he returned to New South Wales leaving behind missionaries untrained in evangelism. They achieved few if any converts and within twenty years three were dismissed for drunkenness or adultery and one "for a crime worse than either".

During the 1820s and 30s, with increasing contact with the Pakehas, the Maoris began to be more and more influenced by Western civilisation. They took to wearing European clothing, both sexes generally smoked pipes, their habits of eating and old customs were either abandoned or modified until in some areas the tribal structure itself was tottering. And with all this change came a catastrophic reduction in the Maori population - a loss of as much as forty per cent. European ailments like whooping cough, influenza, small pox and measles caused great epidemics and loss of life and venereal diseases became very common, adding to the death rate and decreasing the fertility of the tribes.

But the Maoris also slaughtered themselves. They had come to the conclusion that the real god of the white man was the 'pu', the gun, and the pu was the first new god to make converts. In 1815, Thomas Kendal, one of Marsden's missionaries succeeded in publishing a Maori dictionary. Later in 1820 he took two famous chiefs, Hogi and Waikato, to England and, with Professor Lee, a Cambridge linguist, produced a more accurate orthography. In 1821 Hogi set out on his return journey and on the voyage his ship stopped at Sydney. Here he exchanged all the presents he had been given in London for three hundred muskets. When he arrived home he set about terrorising his ancient enemies. He is reputed to have killed a thousand men near present day Auckland, another thousand at the Thames estuary and perhaps twice that number of the Te Arawa tribe on Mokoia Island in Lake Rotorua. The need for 'utu', satisfaction for injuries received or plain simple revenge, led to savage inter-tribal wars in the twenties and early thirties resulting in heavy casualties, and it is thought about forty thousand tribesmen were slaughtered. This would have been an unprecedented toll by the standards of pre-European times when they fought each other with stone age weapons.

A country without civilised law and order such as New Zealand presented a continual source of problems for those countries whose citizens frequently traded there, and both the governments of the

United Kingdom and New South Wales were concerned to protect their subjects from the savagery of the Maoris and also to protect the Maoris from being exploited by a small but violent and brutal minority of their countrymen. The British government enacted a law allowing British subjects to be tried in British Colonial courts for major crimes committed in New Zealand or any other islands subject neither to Great Britain or other civilised powers. But because of the difficulty in obtaining witnesses to such distant crimes, this act proved unenforceable. Eventually, as a result of the recommendation of the Governor of New South Wales, a British Resident was appointed and in 1833 James Busby took up his appointment at Kororareka with instructions to apprehend escaped convicts, to assist settlers and to establish good terms with the Maoris and urge their chiefs to keep law and order. But how was he to undertake this heavy responsibility? No powers as a Magistrate were conferred upon him, nor was he given any military support, so his influence was negligible.

In the Bay of Islands the situation was getting worse, with continual disorder and gunfights; even the British Resident had been attacked. Finally the residents of Kororareka felt something had to be done and they formed a vigilante committee called the Kororareka Association for the preservation of persons and property. Each member was to arm himself with a musket and bayonet, a brace of pistols and thirty rounds of ammunition. A penal code was introduced to deal with theft, non-payment of rent and other specified misdemeanours and a set of punishments drawn up, which included tarring and feathering. This rough-and-ready justice seemed to have some effect, but the settlers still cried out for effective British intervention. But in Britain many felt that colonies were of little value and involved great expense and often unnecessary wars. This was a view close to the heart of the Colonial Office, which during the thirties was involved in wars in South Africa and was facing revolt in Canada and the West Indies.

In 1835 the Resident, James Busby, believing the islands were threatened by foreign intervention, persuaded thirty-five of the tribal chiefs to sign a Declaration of Independence. They declared they were the heads of a sovereign state called the 'United Tribes of New Zealand'

and that they would meet annually to consider the welfare of their realm. In 1837 Busby went further and proposed that these tribal chief now sign a treaty giving Great Britain the power to administer the affairs of New Zealand in trust for its inhabitants. He believed that Great Britain could exercise these responsibilities with a small force of one hundred English soldiers, who he thought would be more than a match for any likely combination of Maoris. But his ideas were considered to be impractical, and the proposals of Captain William Hobson were favoured in some quarters. Hobson had commanded HMS Rattlesnake, sent in 1837 to protect settlers at the Bay of Islands during inter-tribal wars. He suggested that Britain should, by negotiation, acquire jurisdiction within restricted areas, which should be purchased from the tribes. His ideas bore fruit and in August 1839 Hobson set out from Sydney for New Zealand to negotiate with the Maoris for the recognition of the Queen's sovereignty over the whole or any parts of the islands which they were willing to place under her Majesty's dominion. He was also given permission to annex the South Island by right of discovery.

On 29th January 1840 HMS Herald brought Captain Hobson to the Bay of Islands and on the next day he invited everyone, Maori and European alike, to meet him in the church at Kororareka where he read a proclamation announcing that he had been appointed Lieutenant-General of any territory which may be acquired for the Queen. He called a meeting of chiefs and within a few days they gathered at Waitangi where, in a marquee erected on the lawn in front of the Residency, Captain Hobson addressed them and presented his proposals. The debate lasted all day and in the evening they retired across the river to continue their discussions, when Chief Tamati Waka Nene spoke in favour of accepting the proposals and many agreed with him. The following day, the 6th February 1840, Hone Heke was the first of forty-six chiefs to sign the Treaty of Waitangi, which officials later carried around the country so that eventually over five hundred Maoris could add their mark, though a few refused. By this treaty the chiefs ceded their sovereignty to the Queen and she in return guaranteed the Maoris the lands, forests, fisheries and other property they possessed.

The chiefs also gave the Queen the sole right to purchase their lands and in return the Maoris were given the rights and privileges of British subjects.

On 21st May 1840, Hobson, in his capacity as Lieutenant-Governor of this fledgling British Colony, proclaimed sovereignty over the whole country, the North Island on the grounds of cession by treaty and the South Island by right of discovery. Other notable events of 1840, which help to put these events into context, were the institution of the penny post in Britain. In this year also the young Queen Victoria married her beloved Prince Albert of Saxe-Coburg-Gotha, the "Opium Wars" with China began, Canada gained its own responsible government, and the very last convicts were sent to New South Wales.

When at the end of our journey north we arrived in the bay, we stayed at a hotel in Paihia, the main tourist resort for the area and an excellent base from which to visit all the attractions. One of the most important historical sites in the Bay must be the Treaty House, as Busby's Residency has become known. It stands alone on a bluff overlooking the bay, with a huge lawn in front, where the marquee stood; and marking the spot where the Treaty was signed is a truly massive flagstaff. The house is one of the country's oldest surviving buildings and portrays the simplicity of English Georgian architecture. It was designed by John Verge, the Colonial Architect in New South Wales, and the frame, made of Australian hardwood was shipped from Sydney in 1833 in HMS Imogene. The house was completed in 1834, using bricks made in Australia for the chimney and local woods for the weatherboarding and shingles. In 1870 the house was extended but later sank into a state of decline until 1932, when the Governor-General, Lord Bledisloe, bought the house and grounds and gave it to the nation. The house has since been restored and its rooms are now full of furniture of the period. Its beautiful position with fine views across the bay is enhanced by the gardens which surround it. As we sat on the lawns enjoying the scene, I thought of those forty-six Maori chiefs who signed the treaty a century and a half ago. They must have wished that those white sails that brought the Pakehas to these islands could have found some other land and no doubt they wished, as we all do at some time, that they could return to their old habits and customs. Many passionate statements and heated arguments must have been heard in the seclusion of their discussions across the river that night. And I wondered did Chief Hone Heke, who was the first to sign, make the right decision?

Some distance to the north of the Treaty House is the Meeting House. The Whare Runanga, as the Maoris call it, is a mark of tribal prestige and symbolises a tribal ancestor. The carving at the apex of the roof represents his head, the ridgepole his backbone, the bargeboards his arms, the rafters his ribs and the interior of the house his chest. The meeting house normally displays only the carvings of the local tribe, but the meeting house at Waitangi is unique as carvings from many tribes are incorporated in its decoration. This was done to symbolise the unity of the tribes on that historic day in 1840.

Not far from the beach, appropriately called Hobson's Beach, is the Canoe House. This for me was one of the most exciting things to see in the Waitagi National Reserve, for it houses a magnificent Maori War Canoe. Dug out of three separate trees, with bow and stern sections joined to the main hull by mortise and tenon joints, its single hull is 117 feet long. Though it is not an ancient relic it is built in the traditional way, with a bow piece carved with a grotesque head with protruding tongue and a raked stern piece and, to give it more freeboard in rough water, gunwhale strakes are sewn along the sides of the hull. Built out of kauri it was completed in 1940 for the centennial celebrations, and sits on a wheeled carriage leading down to the water. The sight of it stirred my imagination. It seemed so eager, almost impatient to be launched, and its beautiful pointed paddles, hanging in rows around the walls, were clearly waiting to propel it with pent-up fury and savage intent against some unsubmissive tribe. But nowadays it has to be patient and a lot more conciliatory too, for it's only launched once a year, on the anniversary of the treaty, when, manned by eighty Maori "warriors", it is paddled at speed around the bay. What a sight this must be for those gathered each year to commemorate that agreement made on the sixth day of February 1840, but how terrifying in former times to see such a canoe as this, manned by awesome warriors chanting their war-cry, come powering round the point!

But we live in more peaceable times and we had one last visit to make. The visitor centre, which perhaps should have been our first stop, has an audio-visual presentation which describes the events leading up to the signing of the treaty and is well worth seeing. In the hall amongst portraits of the tribal chiefs who signed the treaty, a copy of the document is displayed and it makes fascinating reading.

One cannot visit the Bay of Islands without getting into a boat and fortunately Fullers, the great tour company in these parts, has an excellent boat which takes holidaymakers around the bay. The trip is called the Cream Trip. For over one hundred years Fullers boats have served the local community delivering mail and stores to the island residents and collecting their produce which is mainly milk, hence the name. The boat we caught delivered parcels to some of the islands, but luckily we had no lambs or churns of milk to collect! No doubt other boats do this now. But it is an excellent trip and our skipper had a never- ending fund of knowledge. I don't know how many islands there are in the bay, nor I suspect do the locals, after all first you have to define what you mean by 'island', and some dry land which protrudes above the high water mark is just a rock or two. However, there must be about a dozen which are large enough to be inhabited by man now or at some time in the past.

Our first mail stop was Moturoa Island, which is the second biggest in the bay and is actively farmed, as the sheep which grazed the hillsides confirmed. This should not be confused with Motuarohia Island not far away where Captain Cook, who gave the bay its name, anchored on his first visit in 1769. The names of the islands are all so alike that we had to pay great attention to the skipper's words as close by is similarly named Moturua Island Here the Frenchman Marion du Fresne established his camp three years after Cook's arrival, only to be taken by the Maoris to Assassination Cove on the mainland nearby to be massacred with his men, and have their flesh eaten in June the same year. For a fleeting moment as the sun strayed behind a cloud I saw in my imagination a huge war canoe full of chanting tattooed tribesmen cutting through the water to fall upon those unsuspecting Frenchmen and lead them to their awful fate. But the sun emerged once more and all I could see was this beautiful island with its sandy shoreline and the sea breaking gently on the beach.

The biggest island of them all has by far the most unpronounceable name, Urupukapuka Island. It too is farmed and is also a recreational reserve with beautiful bays. Our boat secured to a jetty on one of the beaches of this unpronounceable island, where the American author Zane Gray had at one time set up camp and hunted big game fish. One of these was the blue marlin, a large powerful fish of about 1,000 pounds or more, with a rounded spear extending from the snout, which is highly prized by sport fishermen. The fish has given its name to the marlin spike, a pointed iron tool used by seamen to separate the strands of rope when splicing.

Not being addicted to sport or even coarse fishing, we were happy to buy our seafood lunch from the restaurant on the beach, before we boarded the extravagantly named Nautilus, a glass bottomed boat decked out to look like a submarine. The two forty-horsepower outboards protruding from the stern gave the game away and bar some great marine tragedy, it was a fair assumption that we would not even reach periscope depth! But we did have a good view of the bottom through the crystal-clear water and once the skipper or his crew had thrown over sufficient bait to the expectant inhabitants, we saw fish a-plenty.

I'm not too good at identifying fish and am much better with birds and was thrilled later in the day to see some little blue penguins, which are about sixteen inches long and must be the smallest penguin to be found in these waters. We were also lucky enough to see some sooty shearwaters. In Stewart Island in the extreme south these birds breed in profusion, where they have acquired the name of muttonbirds. We also thought we might have seen some buller's shearwaters, which are about the same size as the sooties, but have a distinctive white bar on the tail. Though they are widely dispersed throughout New Zealand, their only known breeding place is in the Poor Knights Islands some twenty-eight miles to the east. All shearwaters are wonderful to watch as they skim the wavetops, banking now and then whenever their wingtips seem about to meet the water. Their flight looks effortless and they rarely seem to flap their wings to gain extra lift; clearly they must know all about perpetual motion. The gannets, which always fascinate me as they plunge headfirst from great heights to catch their fish, seemed positively routine after the shearwaters, as did the red-billed gulls and the dainty white-fronted terns. But there's always a thrill when the dolphins appear, especially when they take station just ahead and play tag with the bows of the boat and we were lucky when a school of bottle-nosed dolphins decided to entertain us.

One final picture of that day, which remains in my mind's eye is the R Tucker Thompson, a tall ship with all her sails filled by a good force five wind and moving with an air of purpose through the waters of the bay. Though having a man's name, I must refer to her as she, not only because it's the mariner's custom to give all ships and boats the female gender, but of course because she is a living thing of beauty. The R Tucker Thompson is of recent, though traditional, construction and is named after the man who wanted her built, though sadly he died before she was completed. She is in fact a brigantine, a two-masted vessel square rigged on the foremast and fore-and-aft rigged on the main. I suppose at about fifty feet in length she is about half the size of the good ship Endeavour, which brought Captain James Cook and his crew safely round the world to these islands over two centuries ago. But HMS Endeavour was a barque, that is to say she had three masts, and was square rigged on both fore and main masts and fore-and-aft rigged on the mizzen.

The following day we decided to visit Russell, and in an almost tropical downpour we thought it best to drive the long way round, hoping that the rain would ease by the time we reached our destination. When we reached Opua we continued to Taumarere, where we branched off to the left on to the road to Russell via Karetu. Most of the tourists go by the passenger ferry which runs direct from Paihia or else by the car ferry from Opua to Okaito and not many seemed to be coming our away. Our road, which after Karetu soon degenerated into an unsealed track, wound its way through stands of native trees, with occasional views of the bay and mangrove swamps to our left. We hardly met another vehicle, though now and then we passed a clearing with some animals grazing and perhaps a house or two, but with little signs of life. In the rain and mud, we began to wonder whether we would get through or become bogged down, but eventually we saw a welcome sign to Russell and in our mud-covered car we arrived feeling as if we had just completed a motor rally.

Russell is really the old time Kororareka, the infamous Hellhole of the Pacific. Captain Hobson called his new capital Russell after Lord John Russell, the British Colonial Secretary, and he established this new capital at present day Okiato, where the car ferry from the mainland terminates. However, as it was so remote the capital was transferred some ten months later to Auckland in March 1841. Three years later on 12th January 1844 Kororareka took the now discarded name of Russell and Okiato reverted to its former name. I was told what Kororareka meant, something to do with a penguin if I remember aright, which I suppose is quite apt!

Having unravelled how these names came about, I can tell you that Russell certainly isn't a hellhole any more, just a delightful sleepy little town set in a bay, where the main occupation seems to be fishing, and tourism or just retiring! It has a pub, well I suppose it's really a hotel, but it has a cavernous public bar, where we sampled the patron's brew while we got our bearings. If you want to learn about the past, a good place to start is generally the Church and Christ Church has plenty to tell. It is still the original church, though repaired and modified over the years. It was begun about a century and a half ago, when funds to start the work were raised by public subscription. James Busby was one of the first to subscribe, a Mr Nobody gave a donation of £1, the Reverend Samuel Marsden, who brought the gospel to the country in 1815, also contributed, and so did Charles Darwin and the officers of HMS Beagle. Darwin had previously visited the Galapagos Islands, where the strange fauna inspired him to develop his theories on the evolution of man.

Hardly had the church been built when, it being one of the few sizeable buildings in the town, it was used as a courtroom to try a Maori charged with murdering a European. The local Maoris demanded that the tribal chief should deal with him according to their customs, but this was denied them. An ugly scene broke out and it seemed that there would be fighting and casualties and a boat was sent to Russell (present day Okiato) for the military, but in the end the expected riot did not occur. The accused was found guilty, but died in prison shortly afterwards, before he was due to be executed.

A few years after the signing of the treaty at Waitangi, the Maoris became disillusioned with their lot and, led by Hone Heke, the first of the chiefs to sign the treaty, began to vent their feelings by cutting down the flagstaff flying the Union Jack at Kororareka. The replacement flagstaff met a similar fate and so it continued over the years until 1845, when at dawn on 11th March Hone Heke and his men made a concerted attack. This time a naval detachment from HMS Hazard was on hand to defend the flagstaff and the Europeans, though the sailors were heavily outnumbered by the Maoris. The fighting continued until noon, when the town's ammunition store blew up. Without further supplies of cartridges and bullets, the decision was made to abandon the town, and the residents and naval party were evacuated to the ships in the bay. As they withdrew Heke's men began to sack and loot the town. To drive them away the Hazard turned her guns on the town, but this did not stop Heke from setting fire to most of the buildings. When peace finally descended, the church was one of the few buildings left standing, though it had been badly damaged by gunfire from the Hazard.

After this engagement, which came to be known as Heke's War, the town was abandoned for over a year and the population moved to Auckland as refugees, but in a year or two they gradually returned to rebuild their homes and renew their trade.

We wandered around the little graveyard reading the names and dates on the tombstones. A large stone in a little fenced plot recalls the defence of the town by the detachment from the Hazard and remembers the two Royal Marines and four Naval Seamen who died in the action. Another belongs to Thomas Garrighty, the fourth mate of the American ship Rainbow, who was fatally stabbed in a brawl on the waterfront. Also remembered are four children who died of scarlet fever within a fortnight of each other and a tall monument is dedicated to Chief Tamati Waka Nene, he who helped persuade the other chiefs to accept Hobson's proposals and sign the treaty.

The church is a simple wooden building with white-painted weatherboarding and tall gothic style windows. Proposals were twice made to pull it down and start again, but the townsfolk had come to love their church and plans for a new building were abandoned. So it remains much as it was when it was first built, though it has been repaired many times and now has a little belfry. For some unknown reason the church was built on a north/south axis rather than the traditional east/west. Inside, the simplicity of the building is striking, with a gallery at the end opposite the altar for the organ and choir. The walls are painted white and the window frames blue and there are good old-fashioned pews, which are nice to see as in so many English churches this lovingly fashioned furniture is being ripped out and tossed aside to be replaced with modern chairs. The kneelers, which in the absence of pews are also rapidly becoming redundant in English churches, had all been made over the years by the good ladies of the congregation, and what beauties they are, incorporating the local scenery, bird life and ships of the nineteenth century navy.

You can't go far in this place without stumbling across some reference to Captain James Cook or HMS Endeavour, so we were quite prepared when we went to the museum just opposite. And sure enough we weren't disappointed, for there in a wing built specially for it stands a one-fifth scale model of the Endeavour, which in real life had an overall length of 98 feet, a beam of 29 feet and needed 15 feet of water in which to float. Standing looking at that beautiful model, it made me wonder at the skill and fortitude of Captain Cook and his men in bringing their ship through uncharted waters and unpredictable weather half way round the world, depending only on the wind for propulsion and the stars to find their way. Neither did they have any means of urgent communication with their base to summon help or spares. No satellite communications for them, their problems were their very own and no one else could help them.

Though to my mind the other exhibits were somewhat overshadowed by the Endeavour, we spent a happy hour looking at the relics of the early settlers and the whaling folk. The rules for the office staff of Salmon & Spraggon Ltd in 1852 were on display. Their office hours were from 7 a.m. to 6 p.m. and they started the day with daily prayers. Though a stove was provided to heat the office, each member of staff was expected to bring 4lbs of coal each day during cold weather. No talking was allowed at work, nor could staff leave the room without permission. Calls of nature were to be satisfied in the garden below the second gate. A scale of pay indicated that children were employed and that boys up to eleven years would be paid one shilling and four pence a week. The rules ended with the statement that: "The owners recognise the generosity of the new Labour Laws, but will expect a great rise in output of work to compensate for these near Utopian conditions". Obviously the call for greater productivity is nothing new!

As we left Russell we felt that we had perhaps gained just an inkling of what it must have been like to have lived in Kororareka during the second half of the nineteenth century, when the New Zealand of today was being formed. Setting this against the background of our modern, comfortable and gadget-strewn lifestyle, one is left with a very great admiration for these early settlers.

We took a short cut home and caught the car ferry at Okaito, which had originally been given the name of Russell and for ten months had had the glory of being the nation's capital. It is now an insignificant place whose only feature of note is the ferry slipway!

Chapter Seven

THE DEPARTURE OF THE SPIRITS

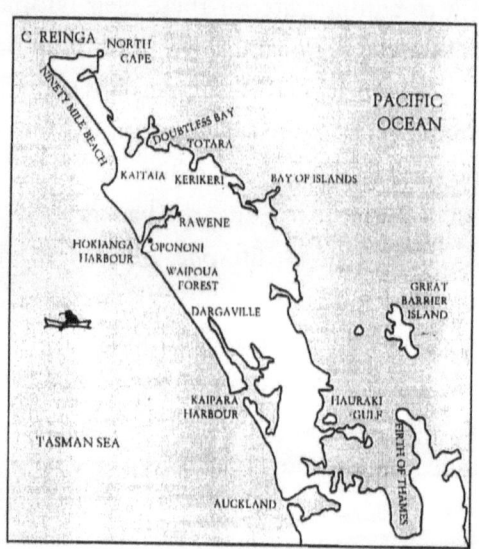

CAPE REINGA AND NINETY MILE BEACH

Our plan on leaving Paihia was to visit the most northerly point of the North Island, Cape Reinga, where the lighthouse stands guard on this needle-sharp headland which juts out into the Pacific. From this remote point where the Tasman Sea and the Pacific Ocean meet, often in a flurry of angry water, the Maoris believed the spirits of their dead departed on their lone, journey back to the ancestral home, Hawaiki. From here too, or more precisely from a land spit just south of North

Cape, those bar-tailed godwits that had humbled us so much when we met them in the Firth of Thames, gather and ready themselves before setting off on their long flight to Siberia. Cape Reinga is often the first landfall made by ships as they approach from the north and must be a welcome sight to the Whitbread Round the World Race yachts as they round the point and make for their third stopover of the race in Auckland.

We drove once more through the Waitangi National Reserve taking the back road to Kerikeri, which is surrounded by huge orchards often protected by windbreaks of Leylandii. This is the home of the Kiwi fruit, otherwise known as the Cape Gooseberry, which was so successfully marketed by the Kiwis around the world. It was the fruit growers of New Zealand, who you may remember sponsored that great sailing catamaran named ENZA, which, with Peter Blake from NZ and Robin Knox-Johnston from UK as joint skippers, took up the challenge to circumnavigate the world without stop in under 80 days. On their first attempt they had to withdraw with storm damage, leaving Bruno Peyron and his crew in Commodore Explorer to complete their circumnavigation in 79 days, 6 hours and 19 minutes, thus breaking the 80 day challenge. With ENZA both lengthened and strengthened Peter Blake and Robin Knox-Johnson set off again in 1993 from Southampton and brought ENZA into Brest to beat the previous record by clocking up a new time of 74 days, 22 hours, 17 minutes and 22 seconds. A great record for the Kiwis, which I hope gave a big boost to New Zealand fruit sales. I wonder if it did?

We approached Kerikeri down a long straight road with citrus and other orchards on each side to find a modern town with a good modern shopping centre. Luckily shopping is fairly low down on our priority list so we drove through until we reached Kerikeri inlet and suddenly we felt as if we were in Cornwall. With yachts and fishing boats swinging at their moorings against a lovely backdrop of trees, we could have been in some backwater of the Fal, but in fact we were at the end of a creek off the Bay of Islands. And there just behind the quay was this big stone house, which looked as if it could have been built with granite from Bodmin moor.

Here at the head of the creek, Samuel Marsden, yes, he who preached the gospel for the first time on New Zealand soil on Christmas Day 1815, set up his second mission station. A wooden house, it was built in 1821 in the Georgian style, with a covered veranda on the ground floor and was the home of the local missionary, until in 1832 it was given to the mission blacksmith, a Mr James Kemp, after whom it takes its name, Kemp House. No doubt in those days the blacksmith had an very important job in the community as a great many of the farming and other tools were made by him for the locality. So perhaps he deserved such a splendid residence, which served him and his descendants until the mid-1970s, when it was gifted to the NZ Historic Places Trust. It is now open to visitors and is furnished with the Kemp family possessions, which belong to the period.

Next door is the big stone building, which served as the Mission storehouse. Work started on this beautifully proportioned house in 1832 and it was completed four years later. The stone used must be some form of ironstone as it has a nice red hue, but the lintels, jambs and quoins are in a contrasting creamy coloured stone. The ground floor is still used as a local store, but its merchandise is mainly directed at the tourists. At one time a room on the first floor served as the library for the local Bishop, but though we could look around the shop, unfortunately the two upper floors were not open to visitors. Both these buildings have the distinction of being the oldest wooden and stone buildings in the country. It made me wonder what was the oldest building in UK, possibly the fort built by the Romans at Porchester in Hampshire, but it makes one realise how recent is the history here in New Zealand, which makes it so much easier to relate to!

We retraced our steps through the citrus orchards and joined Highway 10 at Waipapa and soon we were approaching Whangaroa Harbour, where we turned off the main road, and following a narrow lane, we stopped at a little village called Totara, where we were able to survey the rocky peak called St Paul, one of twelve which dominate this almost land-locked harbour. It is a beautiful peaceful place and it filled our hearts with great contentment; yet this was the scene of a great tragedy, which received world-wide publicity at the time and caused a great sense of shock and revulsion in all those who read about it.

It concerns a ship called the Boyd, which anchored here in 1809 and among whose crew was a Maori called Tara. The ship's master, Captain Thompson, had had Tara flogged for some misdemeanour and the local tribesmen heard about this hideously cruel treatment, no doubt from Tara himself. When Captain Thompson and some of the crew were ashore looking for timber for spars, they were set upon by the local tribesmen and all were killed. The tribe then attacked the Boyd and killed all but four of the crew and passengers before the gunpowder keg ignited, causing the ship to catch fire and sink. After the massacre a great ceremonial feast took place when the bodies of the dead mariners were eaten by the tribe. Only four people escaped: one was an apprentice, who had hidden in the hold, and the others were a mother and her two children, who had taken refuge with Maori women. The news spread to the outside world, when the survivors were rescued by a passing ship and taken to Sydney. Shortly afterwards a similar fate befell a ship wrecked off Cape Brett, the southern headland which forms the Bay of Islands.

Perhaps the flogging of Tara in those days was justified. Who can tell? And though flogging to us nowadays in our more enlightened society is repellent, in the nineteenth century it was widely accepted as a suitable punishment, especially at sea, where a master had to maintain his authority unaided and at times could be under threat of mutiny. But no doubt the treatment of crew members and especially the Maoris was often excessive, even by the brutal standards of the time. Both in England and New South Wales there was much concern about protecting British subjects from Maori savagery, and the Maoris from the cruel treatment they often received from the Europeans. But what could be done about it?

Much thought had already been given to this problem and shortly after the Boyd incident the New South Wales government enacted legislation to require ships leaving Sydney, bound for any destination in the South Seas, to deposit a bond of £1,000 as security for good behaviour. I tried to think what £1,000 in nineteenth century money is worth in the 1990s. Perhaps twenty thousand pounds? But whatever it is worth today, it must have been a very great deal of money. But sadly it is doubtful whether the measure, though full of good intent, had any real influence on the behaviour of British masters or the Maoris it was designed to protect.

Happily, today the descendants of the settlers and the Maori tribes seem to live together in harmony in Whangaroa, which gives the impression of being a sleepy little place, where in the main the livelihood of the residents is bound up with the sea and the land which surrounds the harbour.

As we drove out of the village one small shop did catch our eye. Perhaps it was because on the verge outside it had a hovercraft for sale! Not a very big one, but a hovercraft all the same. We really weren't in the market for hovercraft despite the bargain price, but were fascinated by the shopkeeper's main stock. He was a sea shell specialist and he seemed to have every possible sort of shell on display. The very rare were not for sale and some that were, were not cheap. But then we know little about these works of art, which nature produces in such abundance, though they were all labelled with their strange names. We can understand how people can make this an absorbing hobby and ever since we do occasionally search for shells, when we are strolling along a beach, but then the sea birds distract us and our eyes take in a different view and so our collection grows very very slowly.

Leaving Totara, and all thoughts of Tara's revenge behind, we regained the main road and drove through Mangonui, another snug little harbour at the southern end of Doubtless Bay, which in former times was a whaling base. Then at Awanui we turned off Highway 10 and took the little road for Cape Reinga. The land here is very flat and the scenery quickly becomes dull and uninteresting and we were conscious that we were driving on a narrow spit of land, in places no more than two or three miles wide. Soon we began to feel like the spirits of those long dead Maoris and thought we also might soon be leaving for the land of Hawaiki! We really did find it a monotonous drive and when we arrived at the metropolis of Pukenui, which has a few houses and a pub, we had developed a great thirst. Our timing was fortunate as this is New Zealand's most northerly pub, and who knows, we could have driven on without realising the danger! The pub is a free house run by Norm MacDonald and his charming wife, who insisted on taking a photograph of us both on the bench outside. We were the only customers (perhaps we were between tourist coaches), but Norm insisted that life here is busy and he thought life in Auckland must be a doddle! He also has a panel-beating business and, as people tend to run out of petrol on this road, he keeps a little petrol in jerry cans to rescue the stranded. In fact I think he and his wife act as a general Aunt Sally for tourists and locals who travel along the road.

Though we were fortified by good ale, or perhaps because of it, we found that our enthusiasm for seeing the Cape with its lighthouse had evaporated. We had seen many such lighthouses in our travels and rightly or wrongly we decided to give it a miss. Retracing our steps a mile or two, we found a pleasant spot at the mouth of the Houhora harbour overlooking the sands at low water. This is another of New Zealand's well protected inlets, which must make this coast a lovely place for sailing.

The road north to the Cape runs up the north-eastern side of the peninsula and on the south-western side is the Ninety Mile beach, the one place where we were not allowed to drive our hire car. Though called Ninety Mile beach, it is in fact only fifty-six miles long. How this discrepancy came about I don't know, but it is nevertheless a good descriptive name for this beach which seems never ending. We made a detour to visit the beach and it gives you an incredible feeling of space. The sand is like fine pepper and the sea is very shallow for a long way out. We saw a horse standing in the water at least a quarter of a mile out and his belly was still clear of the water. And though it was a fine day, with good visibility, the beach to our left and right extended into the far distance and vanished in a heat haze. It is backed by high sand dunes and Abel Tasman, the Dutch navigator, referred to this as a desert coast. Fullers, the tour company we met at the Bay of Islands, run a coach tour to Cape Reinga, which returns along this beach. Their coaches have four wheel drive and the drivers know where the dangerous quicksands are. Private cars are, however, strongly discouraged from using this route. I would like to have seen a chart of this coast, which must be difficult for the mariner with its shallow waters and low featureless coastline.

Heading south once more we took Highway 1 at Awanui and passed through Kaitaia, a sprawling town, which must be the main commercial centre for this northernmost area. Once clear of the town we began to negotiate one hairpin bend after another as the road climbed up over the Maungataniwha range, covered with native bush, until we reached the summit at about 1,300 feet, where we had superb views of the area. When we had finished our descent, we left Highway 1 at Mangamuka Bridge and took the little road which follows the Mangamuka river on its journey, among the mangrove swamps, to Hokianga harbour.

The mangrove family of trees are evergreen and grow in estuaries between the high and low water levels with their heavy branches spreading far above the reach of the highest tide. Their roots can radiate as much as eighty feet from the trunk and lie just below the surface and produce erect peg-like rootlets which are alternatively exposed to the air or immersed in water. They have a special function to carry air down to the main roots in the waterlogged mud below, which is a world of its own with crabs, eels, oysters, hoppers and insects galore.

Our road took us to a tiny settlement called Kohukohu, with a little slipway from which the ferry makes its hourly trip across the water, to Rawene. While awaiting its departure we chatted to a social worker, who was doing her rounds, which seemed to cover a very large area. She was a first-generation Kiwi, whose parents were from Liverpool and Blackpool, and now lives in Rawene and was obviously very proud of her country. We commented upon the number of corrugated tin roofs we had seen on the houses and she surprised us by saying that even now many houses rely on the rainwater they catch on their roof for their domestic supply. This is often drained into a number of tanks to build up a reserve. If they do run short of water in a dry spell, she told us, they buy water from the local authority and it is delivered by road bowser. As we thought, many of these tin roofs are well insulated, which helps to keep the heat in during winter and out in summer, and this insulation also reduces the noise level when it is raining hard.

Rawene is a former timber town and all its streets seem to be climbing up or coming down a hill, which must have kept its residents fit in former times. Nowadays it wouldn't make a jot of difference as no one seems to walk when the car is handy. It's a strange though picturesque town and one wonders why it was necessary to build some of its shops and houses out on stilts in the river. Perhaps they had difficulty clearing the land, but one would have thought that a timber town would be well equipped to deal with trees and scrub. We were mystified! It has an attractive-looking church, and the other building which caught our eye was Clendon House, with a pleasant covered veranda at the front and a freshly painted red corrugated iron roof. It was built in the 1860s by James Clendon, the local magistrate, and bought by the Historic Places Trust in 1972 and is now open to the public, but we were running late and had to give it a miss.

Our destination was Opononi, a little village almost at the mouth of Hokianga Harbour. Opononi, what an odd sounding name! But then many names in New Zealand are real tongue-twisters and often strange to our ears and it's always fun to discover how they came about. Apparently back in the summer of 1955/56 a dolphin began to be a familiar sight in the shallow waters of the harbour and this friendly mammal played ball with the children and, so they say, some even had a ride on her back. The dolphin got the name 'Opo' and the village seems to have changed its name in her memory. Indeed there is a fine stone sculpture of a dolphin and a boy in her memory outside the one hotel in town, where we arrived rather late in the day hoping for a room. One couple were at reception as we arrived and, believe it or not, they got the very last room. But the lady proprietor was very comforting and assured us she could find us a room somewhere in the area. After several telephone calls and what seemed an eternity to us tired travellers, she had to admit defeat, but with an expansive smile on her face she offered us backpackers' accommodation. To my dear wife, who had visions of a leisurely bath and a relaxing whisky in the seclusion of a comfortable bedroom, this was not the best news. However it was Hobson's choice and we were grateful for a bed. When we saw our simple though tiny room, with its double bed, small wardrobe and hand basin, we were pleasantly surprised and of course the bill was pretty minuscule. But we did have to share the loos and washing facilities and though we had the use of the communal kitchen we decided we would at least luxuriate in the restaurant, where we thanked our kind proprietor for doing her best.

As we first approached Opononi it had appeared that the big hill on the other side of the creek was covered with ripe wheat, so golden did it look in the evening sun. But as we got nearer we could see it wasn't wheat, it was sand, the whole hill was just plain sand. It really was a quite unforgettable sight. This is a huge sand dune, sculptured by the wind as in a desert and like its cousins in the Sahara, it too is on the move and slowly but surely is devouring the land around it. The locals told us that somewhere in that sand are a tractor and a car which are recent victims, and I daresay there are many other interesting relics which may come to light as ancient artefacts in some future century.

In earlier times Hokianga harbour was busy with the timber trade which centred on Rawene a few miles upstream. But since the 1920s, when the indiscriminate felling of the kauri tree was stopped, the trade has fallen off and the sand has built up, forming a bar at its entrance and shallows in the harbour, which is dominated by that enormous sand dune. Now the harbour is a summer resort, where children play with bucket and spade and the more adventurous, venture onto the water to sail their dinghies in the lee of the dune.

The following morning, after a good bacon and egg breakfast, which we felt went with our new, though perhaps bogus, status as backpackers, we took the road to Omapere further along the river and then climbed up and away from the sea. At the top we stopped for one, last look at Hokianga harbour, with the water glistening in the sunlight and the shoals and channels showing clearly. At the entrance the Tasman sea was calling up its foam-crested breakers in its ceaseless attack on the bar, and there above it all was this enormous sand dune, oblivious of the sea and intent on waging its own slow and remorseless battle with the land below.

Soon we were following the course of the Waimamaku river as we drove along State Highway 12 towards the Waipoua Forest, which is famed for the kauri tree, whose botanical name is agathis Australis. We began to climb and had our last view of the plains before our view became obstructed by trees and shortly afterwards we ran out of road. Our beautiful State Highway 12 with its lovely tarmac surface had suddenly degenerated into a gravel-strewn track! But within a few hundred yards we saw the road construction men and not far away State Highway 12 resumed its polished image, but only for a mile or so as we wound our way through the forest. Then once more the metalled surface gave way to granite chips, which our poor tyres pushed into the mud as we ground slowly forward.

There wasn't much traffic about and with these giant trees on either side the unsealed road took on the appearance of a forest track. We began to feel that for the first time we might perhaps be seeing the land the Moa Hunters and certainly the early Maoris might have known. The largest kauri tree in this forest, which has been named Tane Mahuta, is 167 feet tall; quite a giant, but certainly not one of the world's tallest. The tallest tree in UK for instance is a Grand Fir, which graces Leighton Park, Powys, with its lofty 203 feet, but then it's not a native.

What makes the mature kauri so unforgettable is its enormously thick trunk; the one just mentioned has a girth of nearly 57 feet, and their trunks go straight up perhaps to as much as 60 feet before they start branching, when they produce a round sort of mop head. As we looked at one of these giants, I found myself trying to estimate how many planks of wood it would produce but it was a mind-boggling exercise, which I soon abandoned. But I could begin to understand why it was that ships would come to this remote land with its strange people in search of this timber, which is both light and durable with an attractive creamy brown colour. The wood is also remarkably free of knots and other defects and according to Thomas Kirk, who wrote Forest Flora of New Zealand in 1889, is tougher and more elastic than American spruce and more easily worked than Californian Redwood and was used for boat building and general construction purposes. The younger trees, which cast their branches off as they grow like church spires in the forest, are called 'rickers' and these were eagerly sought as they were ideal for ships' masts and spars.

The kauri belongs to the pine family and like all its cousins it exudes a resin, which solidifies into a beautiful clear golden gum, which is used as a basis for varnish. The Maoris and later the Pakehas also carved figures and ornaments from it which can be highly prized, and kauri gum from ancient decayed forests, known as gumfields, was mined for this trade. A piece of kauri wood from a gumfield near Whangarei has been carbon dated and is estimated to be over 34,000 years old!

The gumdiggers gave their name to a lightly-branched shrub that grows in the vicinity of the kauris. The blossom of this shrub, whose botanical name is pomaderris kumeraho, if rubbed between wet hands makes a lather and for this reason it became known as Gumdiggers' soap.

Kauris have a very long natural life - the great Tane Mahuta is thought to be about 1,250 years old and it's still going strong. He must have seen some grand sights in his time. I expect he was on good terms with the moas, when they were grubbing at his feet for food and knew and tolerated the Moa Hunters and the Maoris, but he's probably very thankful that he didn't make the acquaintance of those white-faced newcomers, at least not until very recently, when they seem to have become a little more sympathetic to his lifestyle!

We continued our drive through the forest, passing the odd construction gang, who were labouring to widen the track or straighten a sharp bend, and then the road narrowed again and ahead we could see it taking a sort of side-step to the right as it bent its way between two massive trees, which looked like some giant's gateway! And in fact it was a sort of gateway as very soon we were leaving the forest and feeling the benefit of the midday sun.

A visit to Matakohe, a farming settlement just off the main Dargaville road is a must. Here the kauri tree was once the centre of a thriving industry based on these magnificent forest giants, which until the arrival of European settlers some 150 years ago had remained untouched for tens of thousands of years. Now it is estimated that less than four per cent of virgin kauri forest remains in the whole of the

North Island and as a kauri takes some 500 years to reach maturity, the creation of a new forest is well-nigh impossible. But Matakohe is doing its best to keep alive the colourful story of these great forests and has established a Kauri Museum which paints a fascinating and humbling picture of life among the bushmen and gum-diggers who tore a living from the wild, unforgiving forests and swamps at the end of the nineteenth and beginning of the twentieth centuries. The enormous amount of work in felling these giants, without the aid of the modern day forester's chainsaw, is brought home. It took a team several days to cut a big tree down and then it had to be cut up into manageable lengths before being moved to the mill. Often they could roll the logs downhill from where bullock teams would pull them to the river. Sometimes they would roll them to the bottom of a gully, which they would then dam and fill with water so that the logs floated. When all the logs were in, the gate in the dam would be released and the logs would be sucked through into the river and thence down to the mills. Truly a Herculean task, which gave employment and prosperity to the locality and continued until recent times, as photographs of bulldozers being used to move these huge logs testify. Though we now moralise about the decimation of the kauri forests and the spoiling of the environment, for those early settlers, struggling against the elements in a strange and often inhospitable land, it was a legitimate use of available resources to provide money to feed and house their families. Among the fascinating exhibits, photographs and reconstructions in this museum is part of an ancient kauri recovered from the swamp and thought to be forty-five thousand years old. And there's kauri gum, also from the swamp believed to have been formed about forty-three million years ago, give or take a few million!

After visiting this museum one can begin to appreciate the wonder of these few remaining kauris and understand why their conservation is so important and to feel thankful that the Kiwis take it so seriously.

Soon our road ran alongside the Kaihu river and the numerous road signs told us we were in Kumara country. The Maoris who came in their fleet of canoes in the mid-fourteenth century brought with them many cultivated food plants from their homeland. Those that survived the transplanting are thought to include yam, gourd and kumara, which we know as sweet potato. The kumara was the most successful of the three and is widely cultivated in both islands. I remember at one stop we saw kumara chips being sold! We tried them and I thought they were rather unusual and a real monument to the culinary enterprise of the Maori and Anglo-Saxon!

The kumara fields dwindled and we entered the outskirts of Dargaville, not the most memorable town, but whose main shopping street could do as a setting for High Noon! Without the cars parked in a solid row on either side of the street, I could see Gary Cooper with his firm jaw standing at one end with both hands poised for the quickest draw in the West! We needed some sandwiches for lunch and we asked a cheerful young girl in the baker's shop how does one say the word Dargaville? Does one use the French pronunciation? Perhaps it was a stupid question and I had forgotten that French isn't really taught in most schools here, and quite rightly so, but she said, "We call it Dargaville," and the French would have been proud of her!

The founding father of the town, one Joseph McMullen Dargaville, was an Aussie of Irish descent, though there must have been some French blood coursing through the family veins. He came here in 1872 to trade in kauri timber and kauri gum, which was shipped down the Wairoa river to that immense stretch of water called Kaipara Harbour, which is about forty miles long. It has a huge number of inlets which infiltrate the surrounding country, and before the roads and railways were built, must have had many places where ships and boats could load timber and gum and unload supplies. The great size of this harbour is brought home when one learns that its coastline is more than two thousand miles long. The bar at the entrance was always a great danger to sailing ships and steamers, especially the former, and many came to grief in storms and their skeletons can still be seen at low tide. With better internal communications the water-borne trade dwindled, though the regular steamer, which ran between Hellensville in the south and Dargaville in the north was only phased out as recently as 1940.

We drove round this great natural harbour and at Wellsford, feeling sad to lose contact with it, we branched off onto Highway 16 for Helensville. At Wellsford, which was originally a gum-digging settlement, the locals rebelled against the Maori name, unpronounceable Whakapirau, and with great ingenuity invented a new name for their town. They called it Wellsford, using the initial letters of their surnames, Watson, Edgar, Levet, Lester and so on. Unfortunately we don't seem to have the surnames which gave the last five letters. What a pity!

As we left Helensville and drove through the vineyards near Kumeu we began to feel the presence of the country's largest city. Our route became busier, with ever more traffic joining from side roads, and with more and more modern housing the scenery took on a suburban air as we came upon Birkenhead. No ship builder's slipways with hammer-head cranes met our eyes, nor did we hear the scouse's accent, for this is a sunnier version with a holiday air about it, where tourists caravans are seen.

And so once more we entered Auckland as we prepared to swap our hire car for seats on the train to continue our journey south to Wellington and across the sea to the Southern Alps.

Chapter Eight
THE OVERLANDER

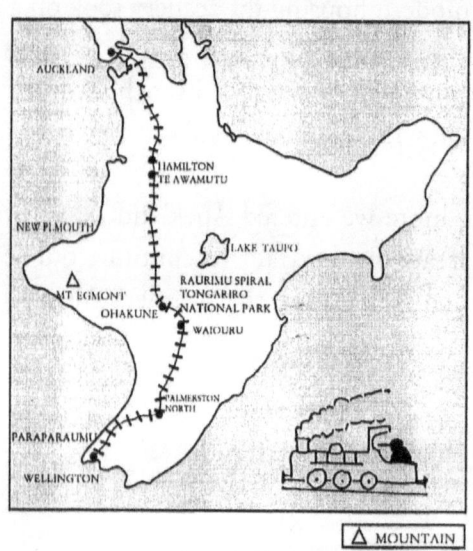

ROUTE OF THE OVERLANDER

In our present day society, speed and convenience seem to be the most important factors when we think about our travels. For long distances we have to go by air; gone are the leisurely days when we could afford five weeks for the voyage from UK to New Zealand. Now we squeeze ourselves into jetplanes and make the trip in a day or so. Nobody really knows how long it takes as we all get muddled with the time zones and arrive at the other end, unsure of the time or even date! For shorter distances we choose the car, for door-to-door convenience, and travel in isolation from our fellow beings in our own little capsule and competing with others for road space.

In my youth the railways were still king and with careful study of Bradshaw's Railway Guide, one could travel the length and breadth of UK, perhaps with one or two changes of train and in the company of one's fellow man, to whom, contrary to general belief, one did talk. Furthermore one had the time to enjoy the particular scenery which only the rail passenger could view as he travelled along the way reserved especially for trains. Breathtaking views of valleys, rivers, mountains and seashores were interspersed with the backs of houses and dreary industrial sites, which one could examine at leisure or ignore, as the mood required.

So with a desire to experience once again the more leisurely travelling of our youth, we decided we would travel to Wellington, our next port of call, by New Zealand Rail.

New Zealand's rugged bush clad hills made transport difficult for the early European settlers. Tiny remote pioneer communities were served only by bullock wagons, river barges and coastal vessels subject to the vagaries of tide and weather. The railway, which was to provide the vital communication link to develop the country, was built by private capital on a piecemeal basis as demand arose, starting in the 1860s. It operates to this day on a narrow gauge of 3 feet 6 inches, half that of the original track used by the old British Great Western, which started off with a 7 feet gauge, though this was eventually changed to conform with the UK standard 4 feet 8 ½ inches. The narrow gauge was an obvious choice in New Zealand, since it made less work when clearing the routes through the bush. By the 1930s, most of the track had been laid in both of the two islands, and the state had absorbed all the railways of importance in the country. Work on the line from Auckland south was started in 1865, but progress was painfully slow and, after fifteen years' toil, had only progressed as far as Te Awamutu some 95 miles to the south. From here on the Maoris were hostile as this was the King Country, and work was abandoned. But in 1884 when relations had improved and Parliament had approved the route, work began once more. At the same time, the railway from Wellington to Manawatu was extended northwards, and finally in August 1908, the two tracks met near Ohakune just south of the Tongariro National Park, fittingly about midway between the two cities. In February 1909 the Government purchased the track and the New Zealand Main Trunk service began.

In the great railway building age the big city stations were often like cathedrals built in honour of steam, which was revolutionising transport throughout the world. St Pancras is perhaps the best example, but stations all over the former British Empire followed this trend. Stations at Kuala Lumpur, Delhi and Capetown are fine examples and those in Auckland and Wellington are also impressive buildings marking this great new age. But neither in Auckland nor Wellington were we able to enter the buildings. Nowadays taxis and private cars have direct access to the platform, where passengers claim their pre-booked seats from a check-in desk on the platform itself. The station buildings now stand forlorn, unloved and ignored and, I suspect, will end looking like the many small stations we were to see on our journey south, vandalised, covered with graffiti and often locked and barred.

When we arrived a smart silver diesel train was waiting on our platform, but this was the Rotorua train, appropriately called the Geyserland. It follows the same route as our train, the Overlander, as far as Hamilton when it turns eastwards through the Mamaku Ranges for "Sulphur City". I was chatting to the driver when a commuter train came in on the other platform. He told me that the commuter trains were recent acquisitions and that they had formerly been running around Perth in Western Australia. The commuter train did look a bit second-hand and it made me remember our visit to Perth a year or so ago. I remember how impressed we were by the splendid new train we caught on our visit to Fremantle. Everything was automatic and new and shiny. My friendly train driver looked at his watch, climbed into his cab and off he went. A few minutes later, our train arrived, pulled by two of the ugliest diesel engines I think I have ever seen. Built in Japan, like almost every other mechanical and electronic object here in New Zealand, they looked like overgrown versions of those diesel shunters one sees marshalling wagons in the yards. They were pulling four passenger cars and luckily we were booked into the last one, an observation coach with a splendid wrap round window at its rear end. We had airline-type reclining seats with a folding table and a beautiful window from which to admire the scenery. The train was in fact run like an airliner, with meals and drinks being provided and a running commentary to keep us apace with its progress.

One of our fellow passengers was a railway employee who worked on the engines back in the depot. I knew that the railways, built largely by private capital then nationalised, had once more been privatised, and when I asked him how he felt about this he seemed to accept it as a necessary evil in order to keep them running. But he was very upset that it was now very largely owned by an American company who seemed to want their pound of flesh. Other than commuters in and around Auckland and Wellington, the great majority of its passengers are tourists such as ourselves and all the long distance services are given names, like the two already mentioned, in a grand marketing effort. I was told that the most exciting train is the Transalpine in the South Island, which winds its way from Christchurch through spectacular river gorges and the rugged, snowcapped Southern Alps, before descending into the lush rain forests of the West Coast at Greymouth. So tourist-oriented are these trains that you just cannot buy tickets at most stations: you have to buy them through travel agents. Besides the passenger service, there is quite a lot of goods traffic on this line, mostly in the shape of containers passing backwards and forwards between the two main ports.

We pulled out of Auckland station and passed between warehouses and the backs of buildings and industrial sites, which seem the same the world over, and picking up speed we raced the cars and lorries along the motorway. Then thankfully we began to have our own private world of farms and tiny settlements as we travelled along our single track with only the domestic power lines to keep us company.

We stopped at Hamilton, which is built on the banks of the Waikato River, at 260 miles the longest in New Zealand and along whose banks we had earlier driven on our way to Rotorua. Barely fifteen minutes after leaving Hamilton we were entering the tiny station at Te Awamutu, where the building of the permanent way came to an end over a century ago, for here was the beginning of the King Country, named after the Maori King movement. When the Maori King Tawhiao and his people were forced to move from their land on the banks of the Waikato after the wars of the 1860s, they came here, an area free of Europeans, which they declared was to be theirs. They maintained this as an exclusive Maori territory for several decades until, with the consent of the Maori chiefs, the route for our train was agreed and the Pakehas were gradually allowed into the area. Interestingly, one of the conditions that the Maoris imposed when they agreed that the railway could go ahead, was that no alcohol should be allowed into King Country. Perhaps this indicates the terrible effect that the settlers' rum had had on the Maoris in those early years when huge areas of land were bought by unscrupulous settlers.

Soon we were approaching Raurimu. 'Rau' means many and rimu is one of the native trees. At one time it may have had many rimu trees, but sadly no longer, for this was at one time a timber town where the rimu or red pine was heavily milled for its valuable timber. Luckily, it is still widespread throughout the country and, once seen, can easily be recognised again with its long needle-like leaves hanging down in graceful festoons. But the rimu tree is not what makes this little town famous. The reason why Raurimu is well known is its famous spiral, for here the railway has to overcome the sharp rise onto the central volcanic plateau. By means of two complete circles which burrow in and out of the hillside, the line is lifted about seven hundred feet and, as the train climbs the one in twenty-five gradient, one can see both ends as the train bends around the curves.

At the top the gradient eases as the train runs through the Tongariro National Park, with the snow-clad volcanic peaks of Ruapehu, Tongariro and Ngauruahoe away to our left. As I watched this empty landscape speeding by, I thought what a long-standing problem the land had been in this country since the earliest colonial days. The Maoris originally held most of it, and by the Treaty of Waitangi the Queen guaranteed them all that they possessed and they in return gave her the sole right to purchase any they wished to sell. That was fine in theory, but it didn't quite work like that in practice.

Conscious of this promise and with a humanitarian approach to the Maoris, the first Governor, Captain William Hobson, instituted a scrutiny of pre-Treaty land claims, whether by missionaries, settlers or those distant speculators in Sydney. But the investigations were complicated and seemed never-ending, and the early settlers at best got a feeling of insecurity or at worst became involved in protracted litigation and so relations between the settlers, Governor and the Maoris were often soured.

When Wellington was being built on the original settlement of Port Nicholson, the local Maoris denied having sold their villages which stood in the way of the new town and tried to stop the surveyors. In Nelson also, the Maoris denied having sold the land on which surveying had begun and, in the ensuing confrontation, the surveyors' huts were burnt down. When the authorities tried to arrest the two tribal chiefs responsible, they were attacked and their leader and several Europeans were killed in what became known as the 'Wairau massacre'. In this instance Hobson's successor, Governor Robert Fitzroy, concluded that the Europeans were wrong and that the Maoris had not in fact sold their villages. But while he condemned the Maoris for killing the Europeans, he refused to institute proceedings against them. By this he seemed to be telling them that one wrong does indeed excuse another, a lesson which the Maoris took to heart.

At New Plymouth in Taranaki more trouble was brewing over the Europeans' claim to some 60,000 acres, but this time bloodshed was avoided, though tempers were strained as tribesmen found settlers encroaching on their land. And again the Governor found in favour of the Maoris, but managed to placate the Europeans by negotiating the sale of other lands for the settlers.

These constant quarrels over land were the main cause of the Maori wars, which started at Kororareka when Hone Heke attacked and cut down the flagstaff flying the Union Jack and then sacked and burnt the town. For over a year the north suffered a series of similar sporadic attacks. In one such action a mixed force of infantry, marines and sailors were ordered to make a frontal attack on Heke's fortified village. As they advanced in close formation they were mown down by concealed fire from the Maoris, who were well organised and skilled in the art of ambush. Warfare between the two races continued and trade suffered. But in 1847 the new Governor, George Grey, who was described at the time as 'the great dictator, the great Maori Tamer', showed great ruthlessness and eventually the fighting between Maori and Pakeha stopped, at least for the time being.

When the fighting stopped, Grey restored to the Crown the sole right to purchase Maori land. But the system was still open to criticism because the Government bought land at sixpence an acre and sold it to the settlers for ten shillings or even a pound an acre. The only real benefit was that the sale of the land was now properly recorded, but the Government was in effect robbing the Maoris in order to save them from being swindled by the settlers.

In 1854 troubles began once more in Taranaki, with murders, sieges and skirmishes. The angry and frustrated settlers proposed that the Government should confiscate the lands of chiefs opposed to land sales. However the Governor wisely ignored these proposals and, after much patient negotiation, was successful in buying a strip of coastal land which the settlers had wanted for a long time. But in doing so he encouraged the local Maoris to break a long-standing tribal law, namely that tribesmen could not sell their parcels of land without the approval of the chief.

Once again when surveyors began to mark out the land violence erupted and a war, which was to last some eighteen years, began. The Maoris, unencumbered by baggage and living in the forests where they could eat off the land, had freedom of movement and could harry the settlers when and where they chose. Though the troops took the Maori village of Waitara and set it ablaze, the Maoris in their turn burnt almost every farmhouse in the province and captured most of the stock. Thus the settlers were forced off their lands and back into New Plymouth and many evacuated their women and children across the strait to Nelson.

Eventually the war spread over most of the southern half of the North Island until, at its climax, over three thousand British troops were endeavouring to defeat a determined enemy waging a gorilla war. The fighting was bitter and marred by savagery but the British troops had a great admiration for the fighting skills and courage of the Maoris. As time progressed the settlers became disenchanted with the military effort and demanded more robust action, but the military preferred a cautious approach which kept casualties down.

When the fighting finally came to an end, about two thousand Maoris had been killed for the loss of about one thousand Europeans. Once more the colonisation of the land could be resumed and after 1873, the purchase of land from the Maoris was facilitated by a new law, which proclaimed that land was divided up among all the owners, and was not under the control of the tribal chief. Thus Governor Grey's purchase of land in 1854, which sparked off this second war, seemed to have been legitimised. So now the individual Maori landowner, eager for money with which to buy food, clothes and rum or under duress to settle debts to the storekeeper, could and did sell his parcel of land to the Government agent. As a result land sales accelerated and by the 1880s the Maoris had sold about seven million acres in the North Island alone.

But Maori resentment still exists and it would be foolish to think that problems with the Treaty of Waitangi are a thing of the past. They aren't. The Maoris are now examining the small print and it will be argued over for many years to come.

Now our train drew into Ohakune, where for the first time I noticed that we had a double track, for there alongside us was the Northerner, as the Wellington to Auckland train is called. Here we said goodbye to our train crew as they left us to take the Northerner on to Auckland and their crew joined us to take our train on to Wellington. At this stage we were running a modest twenty minutes late. But now our conductor told us that there was a 25mph speed restriction due to the lines buckling because of the heat. What heat we thought, it really was just a nice summer's day! How do they manage to stop the lines buckling in the burning plains of India? However we had read that

New Zealand Rail had suffered thirteen derailments in the last three months, so perhaps the speed restriction was unavoidable. But worse was to come for whenever we enquired about our progress we heard we were running later and later. We had ample time to inspect, almost tree by tree, the huge man-made forest which feeds a South Korean-owned paper pulp mill, before we crossed the first of several viaducts carrying us over large boulder-strewn river beds below. Both the Rangitikei and Makohine viaducts are about 240 feet high and about 270 yards long, and we had a real feeling of space as we rumbled across.

Now our train had slowed to a snail's pace and we were told we were approaching the scene of the last derailment three days previously. A container train had left the track and twenty wagons had been derailed.

Though the railway gangs had been working full tilt since the accident, we could see damaged wagons still on their side and one great length of bent track pointing to the sky. It must have been some derailment! I tried to visualise the scene and my mind's eye went back to those happy days when my two sons and I played with our Hornby electric train set. We had many derailments, but this was for real: the forces involved must have been huge and the squeal of wheels grinding against the bending rails followed by the thumps as the wagons hit the embankment must have been deafening.

By now we were running about an hour and a half late and still we ambled on at a sedate 25 mph. Perhaps caution was indeed still necessary, but by now our patience was becoming a little worn. Our expected time of arrival was getting later every minute and we were anxious about our friend who was meeting us. But clearly late arrivals are quite normal on New Zealand Rail and they had installed a radio telephone in the bar, which we were free to use to advise our chum of our delayed arrival. But just what was our arrival time? With the aid of the conductor we made an inspired but not very accurate guess.

Were we going a little faster perhaps? Nobody dared speculate, especially the nice lady with two bored and hungry children, whom she had brought along as a treat while her husband and elder relatives made the journey by car. We told her she should qualify for the 'Mum of the Year' award, and while we were discussing the merits of her actions we noticed we really were moving faster. Perhaps with the cool of the evening the danger of track buckling had passed and as we began to pick up speed, we all felt our journey was coming to an end. The countryside softened into bush-clad hills and on our right we had occasional glimpses of the Tasman Sea. Then we were pulling into Wellington, two hours and ten minutes late.

It had been an interesting journey and if we had the opportunity we would like to try the Transalpine – surely they can't get track buckling in the Southern Alps! We had also met some nice folk and after all, as our conductor said, we did better than yesterday's train, they were nearly three hours late!

CHAPTER NINE

CAPITAL CITY

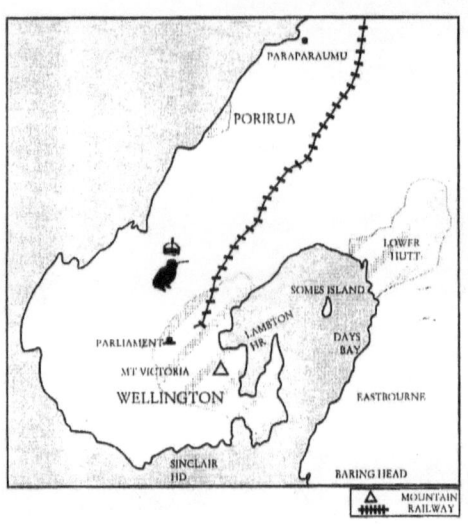

WELLINGTON

Probably the best place from which to view Wellington for the first time is Mount Victoria Lookout, and this is where we were taken by our enthusiastic host as soon as we got clear of the train. The sun was just setting, so it was a glorious time of day to see this magnificent harbour reaching out towards the South Island just over the horizon. Houses nestle in the hills and the native trees which cover them seem to come right down to the water. Below us we could see the lights coming on in the centre of Wellington, with the station and commercial harbour at

Lambton on its foreshore and the White Lady lighthouse flashing her welcome to visiting mariners.

We had met our Kiwi friend when she lived and brought up her family in Hampshire, but now she had returned home and was rightly proud of the city in which she now lived. She had bought a Victorian house which perched on the side of Mount Victoria and was now busy refurbishing and enlarging it. Luckily she was nearing the end of this mammoth task and had time to welcome us for a couple of nights.

Wellington is hemmed in by its huge harbour, with steep hills between it and the Kapiti coast to the west and the Rimutaka range of mountains to the east. Land in the capital has always been short and the original settlement was centred on Lambton Quay, where in 1852 some additional land was reclaimed from the sea. An earthquake a few years later razed many of the buildings and this encouraged further reclamation, which continues to this day with a massive waterfront redevelopment programme. While the centre of town was being developed for commercial interests the population began building its houses on and among the steep hills and out along two valleys. One of these, with the strange name of Hutt Valley, runs northwards from the northern end of the harbour and the other runs north westwards towards the seaside resort of Paraparumu.

With the city jammed as it is between the sea and mountains, many of its streets are steep and wind their way up the slopes. This is unusual in New Zealand as most towns are generally built on a practical but boring grid system. Wellington, the home of the New Zealand Symphony Orchestra, the Royal New Zealand Ballet and the University of Victoria, with its museums and theatres definitely has the style missing in so many of the towns in both islands. Its many modern buildings blend nicely with their older neighbours, and the houses which are tightly packed into streets radiating from the centre are such a delight that one can spend many an hour wandering around them and enjoying the atmosphere. Nearly all the houses are wooden and painted in lovely pastel shades and their architecture varies from Victorian to Edwardian. Often they have grand porches and verandas bedecked with flowers and shrubs.

New Zealand

The shore at Lambton Harbour is the scene of a huge redevelopment designed to accommodate the National Museum, which is scheduled to move from its present site in Buckle Street. Not only is land being reclaimed, but buildings are being moved in true New Zealand fashion.

Anglican Church Rotorua

Angora – Walter Peak High Country Farm

Doubtful Sound

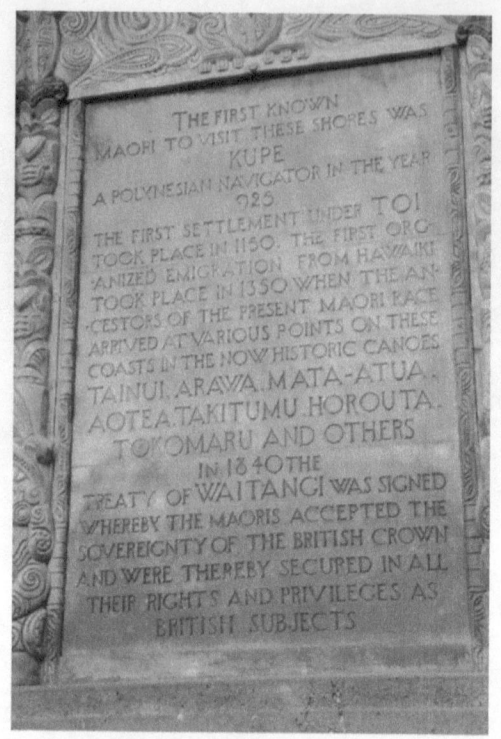

Kupe – the first Maori

Maori Meeting House – Rotorua

Meet the locals

Milford Sound – Mitre Peak

Old St Paul's Church – Wellington

Richard Seddon – Longest serving Prime Minister

The Beehive – Wellington

Typical Town house – Wellington

New Zealand

Wellington Harbour

A fine old stone warehouse had been moved across a street and turned through 180 degrees to make a bigger site for the new museum building and only recently a fine stone Victorian theatre, the Circa, had got up one night and wandered through the town to a more classy area in Taranaki Street. The moves are of course done during the night when traffic is light and streets can be closed. I would love to have seen one of these moves but had to be content with stories of those our host had seen. Three two-storey Victorian-style houses stand in a road close to hers as if they had never been anywhere else. But all are interlopers. They all came at different times and all had to negotiate the same winding route to their new site. The first two made it without too much difficulty, but the third got stuck, wedged on the sharp bend. Undaunted, the removers just cut the house in two and on went the move! We were told that before the house starts on its journey the occupants have to remove breakables, but on the whole the house moves with wardrobes full, curtains up and carpets down and much of the furniture in place. The mind boggles!

We would have loved to have gone to see the used house lots, where one can buy a second-hand house, moved from its old site and awaiting a kindly purchaser to find it a new home. Perhaps if we could move second-hand houses bodily from one site to another we might succeed in getting the UK housing market moving once again! Who knows? If your job moves from say Plymouth to Doncaster perhaps you could then take your house with you. The savings on search fees and conveyancing would surely help pay for the move!

Wellington has been the capital city since 1865 and, with the Beehive forming part of the Parliament buildings, is perhaps one of the most individualistic of all seats of government. The first parliament to meet in Wellington sat in the Provincial Chambers, a wooden building completed in 1857 for the City Council. It was renamed the General Assembly Building and work was started to modify and extend it to include a Legislative Council Chamber and Library and other offices for its national role. This was completed in 1874 and in 1883 further additions were made, this time in brick.

Fire had always been a potent danger in Wellington and in 1907 it struck the General Assembly building and all but the brick additions was gutted. A design competition for the new Parliament building was held in 1911. John Campbell, a government architect, won the design and the foundation stone was laid in 1912, but construction was delayed by shortages of materials and skilled manpower. Eventually in 1918 the Chamber was used for the first time, but the building was not finally handed over until 1922.

Once again the Parliament Buildings are not being used. In 1990 a project was started to restore them and strengthen them to withstand the earthquakes to which Wellington, standing as it does on the fault line, is prone. Great hardened rubber discs are being inserted on strong columns to take the weight of the building and absorb the shock waves. Hopefully the work will be completed in 1995 but until then the MPs have to make do with a temporary Debating Chamber in Bowen House, a modern high-rise building almost next door on Lambton Quay.

Lambton Quay? Surely this should have the odd ship tied up alongside. But not a salt-caked smoke-stack nor a shiny cruise liner did we see! In the early nineteenth century Lambton Quay would have been busy with tall ships loading or discharging cargo amid all the hustle and bustle of a Victorian port. But today the sea has retreated and there are now two other streets between it and Jervois Quay, which now forms the harbour front. Lambton Quay is still busy, but now it is a main thoroughfare. A footplate at the entrance to Bowen House still marks the line of the foreshore in 1840 and in one of the windows the remains of the cellar of an earlier building, perhaps a drinking tavern or hostelry, is still preserved.

The Debating Chamber is open to the public, except when Parliament is in session, and a very charming guide showed us around. One might expect a pretty ersatz room as a temporary expedient, but obviously the honour and prestige of the legislature must be upheld at all times and we were very impressed with its temporary home. The Parliament, which has 99 members is based on the Westminster model, with a Speaker and two Clerks of the Court to advise him or her on procedure. Like Westminster there is a Sergeant at Arms, who carries the Mace, which he lays on the table in front of the Speaker when the House is in session.

When we were there the government was headed by Jim Bolger, the leader of the National Party, who had a one-seat majority, only achieved by appointment of a Labour MP as Mr Speaker. The Government must have carried out its business on a knife-edge, yet nowhere did there seem to be more Thatcherite policies than in New Zealand, and all introduced by the National Party. Perhaps National is Kiwispeak for Conservative!

Comfortable seats and modern wooden desks are laid out in a horseshoe shape for the members and the room is beautifully panelled in native wood, mainly tawa or rimu. With its soft carpeting and microphones at each desk, it must be a delightful place in which to defend one's sacred cows and air one's pet theories.

This beautiful room is a modern replica of the proper Debating Chamber in the Parliament Building just along the way and will become redundant when the Members move back to their refurbished premises.

Recently a new Government has been elected by the new MMP (Mixed Member Proportional Representation) system. In addition to the four main parties, three others put up candidates for election. There was the Christian Coalition, the United Party, and the oddly named ACT! The latter stands for Association of Consumers and Taxpayers and I imagine is somewhat similar to the Ratepayers, which many years ago used to contest local elections in the UK. Under the provisions of MMP, each elector has two votes. One is used to vote for a political party and the other for one on the "list" of candidates. With this system it is quite possible for an elector to vote for one party, say the Alliance, and for candidate of another party, perhaps the Labour party, thus splitting his vote. This is what the pundits expected many electors to do. A poll conducted by Waikato University in conjunction with the New Zealand Herald immediately prior to the election, asked the question, "Which vote do you think will be the most important in deciding which party will get the largest number of seats in Parliament?" Over sixty-four per cent of those questioned thought the party vote was the most important, and this was supported in a later survey of those who admitted they intended to split their vote. So perhaps the Party vote shows the elector's real intention, so what purpose is achieved by the second vote? The uncertainty about the effectiveness of the system in reflecting the will of the electorate had the main parties worried, and a telling newspaper headline after the final televised leaders' debate summed up their mood: "leaders like nervous debs at coming-out ball". So how did it all turn out in the end? Well the electors went to the booths on 12th October 1996 and the results were as follows:

Party	Leader	Seats Won By Party Vote	Seats Won By List Vote	Total Seats
National	Jim Bolger	35	14	49
New Zealand First	Winston Peters	6	11	17
Alliance	Jim Anderson	1	12	13
Labour	Helen Clark	26	11	37
Minor Parties		2	7	9

From the results there can be little doubt the electorate favoured either the National party or the Labour party but many seemed to have hedged their bets by using their second vote to support the next best option. What have they achieved by doing this? No one party has a clear mandate to govern. Was that what they wanted? Do they want a good decisive government or do they want everything decided by compromise? In the event Jim Bolger had the greatest number of seats but no majority, so some sort of coalition government had to be formed. Much negotiating, bargaining and compromise was obviously necessary and eventually, when the terms were right, Winston Peters agreed to support him with his New Zealand First party. But it was not until the second week in December, some two months after the election, that a government could be formed. With a combined strength of sixty-six members the coalition has a majority of seven and Helen Clark of the Labour party is now Leader of the Opposition. Many would say the system has worked well and in the end has produced a majority government, but how long will it be before the New Zealand First hold the National party to ransom by threatening to pull out unless its demands are met? Furthermore it is a complicated system and the ability to split one's vote intentionally or mistakenly, because one is not well-versed in the make-up of the parties, must put in doubt the effectiveness of MMP in reflecting the voters' true wishes. Will those who split their vote come to rue their decision? No doubt time will tell, but New Zealand has a reputation for leading the democratic nations with its many political innovations, such as votes for women and its National Health Service, to name but two. So who knows? Perhaps this brave effort to improve the election process may prove successful and be taken up by other countries. But personally I remain in favour of the "first past the post" system.

On the opposite side of Lambton Quay, where the sea had been in 1840, stands the old Wooden Government Building now being refurbished and modified for use by the Law Faculty of the University. It is a truly elegant building in the Georgian style and one of the largest wooden buildings in the world. The architect had planned that it should have been built in concrete but when tenders were received the lowest was for timber and this was accepted despite the fire risk! Luckily it has survived to date, though it was damaged by fire in 1992. Let's hope that the fire prevention equipment now being installed is equal to the task, as it would be a real tragedy if this beautiful old building was lost.

We walked across Bowen Street, past the Cenotaph and entered Parliament Grounds with the Beehive towering above us on the left and away to the right Parliament House and the General Assembly Library shrouded in scaffolding and plastic sheets. It looked like a construction site, but the Pohutakawa trees were covered with their glorious crimson blossom, the lawns neatly mown and one could visualise how it might look once all the work was complete.

The Beehive, or to give it its official name the Executive Wing provides the government of the day with its Cabinet room, offices for its secretariat and an area where formal dinners and receptions can be held. It was designed in 1963 by Sir Basil Spence, who also designed the post- war Coventry Cathedral and the British Embassy in Rome, to name but two. Work began in 1969 and a plaque records that this building, which looks more like an inverted ice cream tub than a beehive, was opened on 28th February 1977 by Her Majesty Queen Elizabeth of New Zealand. Its unique style is not unattractive and in its way does perhaps act as a symbol of a young, energetic and progressive nation. All the important areas are on an outer ring surrounding a central core, which provides services such as lifts and is clad in marble from the Coromandel Peninsula. On the ground floor, used as a reception area, there is a statue of Kate Sheppard, who led the fight for voting rights for women, which were granted here in 1919. In this respect New Zealand led the world with Great Britain following a tardy nine years later in July 1928. Also displayed are coins of the realm, newspapers and a list of Members of Parliament, which had been buried among the foundations, when work on the new Parliament Buildings was started back in 1912. An interesting time capsule, it will be re-interred in the foundations when the strengthening of the Parliament Buildings is complete.

New Zealand

As we left parliament we met up once again with our friend, who had left us to attend a funeral in Old St Paul's, and as the coast was now clear we went to have a look at this lovely old building. It used to be the Cathedral church of the Anglican diocese of Wellington from 1866, when it was first consecrated until 1964, when the new Cathedral of St Paul's took its place. Old St Paul's is a fine example of the Early English Gothic style adapted to the requirements of a wooden building. When it became redundant there was much soul-searching and agonising and after a ten-year debate the Government agreed to purchase it for the nation. The Friends of Old St Paul's were also formed and they do much to raise funds to maintain the church, which gives so much grace to this area where man is so busy making laws to govern the nation. It is still a consecrated building and is available on an interdenominational basis for weddings and funerals and the like, and it makes a beautiful picture sitting as it does among the trees with its painted exterior and shingled spire. Inside the wooden gothic piers, arches and ceilings give it a warm and mellow air and I was reminded of that other beautiful wooden church which I had visited at Honfleur in Normandy. Nearly all the wood at Old St Paul's is of course native, with rimu and kauri being abundant; but not quite all. The pulpit was carved in England from English oak and was presented by the family of a former Prime Minister of New Zealand, Richard Seddon, who had been born in Eccleston, near St Helen's, Lancashire, in 1845 and who emigrated in 1866. One of the oak clergy stalls was also made of English oak, from carved panels sent from Wells Cathedral no doubt as an expression of unity. What a wise decision it was to save and restore this building which had played such an important part in the spiritual life of early Wellington.

The inner man needed attention and driving up the hill through the picturesque houses we found a bite to eat in the Botanical Gardens in the café by the rose garden. One of the great legacies the British Empire bestowed upon the world was its love for native plants and the Botanical Gardens with which it littered the world. They are fascinating places to visit and offer peace and tranquillity where one can consider the sights already seen and gather strength to renew one's exploration. Though the gardens in Wellington are needless to say hilly, they must be visited, but of course you do need time and two or even three visits are really needed to savour them.

We should have used the cable car to get up to Kelburn, but we had a car and thus forfeited the experience of travelling on a unique service used by millions over the years since it began operating in 1902. However we did enjoy the superb view one gets from the little park at the top. Here one gets a different view from Mount Victoria lookout. Below us was the Basin Reserve, the home of New Zealand cricket and crossing our line of sight were aircraft homing in onto the airport.

We were due to leave for the South Island the following day but we had to find time to drive round the foreshore of this fine harbour, which was formed aeons ago by the flooding of a massive volcanic crater. We drove out along the motorway above the commercial harbour and the railway station, but when State Highway 2 started off for Masterton, we bore right and so down onto the foreshore. We regretfully sped past the Settlers Museum until we reached Days Bay and Eastbourne, where the more affluent have their houses. Some seem to cling precariously to the hillside and to reach them you have to use their private escalators. Others, only slightly more accessible, have narrow driveways piercing the bush, with turntables at the top to help turn your car! Eastbourne is abreast the narrow entrance to the harbour, which the ferries and ships have to negotiate.

Luckily for us the city did not live up to its famous nickname 'Windy Wellington'. Apparently this is well earned as the wind can race through the city sending unsecured items, especially rubbish, flying and knocking the unwary and infirm off their feet. So strong can be the wind, that on one blustery day in 1968, it blew the Wahine, the Wellington to Christchurch ferry, onto Barrett's reef just outside the harbour. After much pounding the Wahine broke free of the reef and drifted into the harbour only to sink with the loss of fifty-one lives. This terrible maritime tragedy, one of the worst in New Zealand's recent history, is depicted in a dramatic model and display in the Wellington Maritime Museum. As one might imagine, this tragic story concentrated our minds as we prepared to set off in the morning, across Cook strait for the little port of Picton, at the head of Queen Charlotte Sound.

Chapter Ten

COOK STRAIT

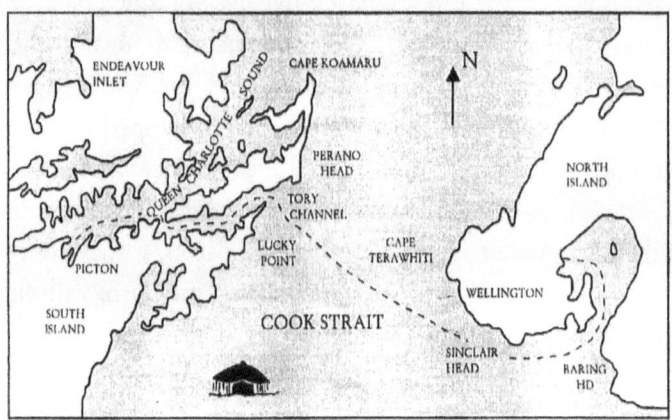

WELLINGTON TO PICTON

Our brief but hectic visit to Wellington had come to an end and daybreak found us setting off for the ferry to Picton. There are now three advertised services which cross the strait, the Interislander, a service run with conventional car ferries, the Lynx, a modern wave-piercing catamaran, and the new Sea Shuttle.

Before we left UK we had booked a passage on the Sea Shuttle, a new fast monohull built in Spain for some twenty two million pounds, which it was claimed would halve the three hour crossing. However we began hearing about its teething problems, with hairline fractures in one of the four jet units, and we were advised to change our booking.

It was a good job we had taken this advice, for two months later when we were about to set off across the strait the new ferry was still not in commission.

Instead we took passage on the Lynx, a modern vessel which emulates much that is bad about airliners and little that, to me at least, is enjoyable in conventional ferries. Sat with about two hundred others in tightly spaced rows, I wondered why the modern travelling public allows itself to be herded into these new vessels, where with a bit of luck you might just be able to see out of a window over the heads of others. All that seems important to the operators of these catamaran-type craft is that you should hear plenty of canned music and be able to feed yourself the whole time with snacks, ice cream, coffee, coca cola or lager: ugh! And if you aren't eating there are the gaming machines to neutralise any thought that the human brain might generate!

Seeing the coastline and the bays, which surely most of us only have a chance to see once or twice, is the least important thing in the minds of the designers and operators. We should have travelled on the Interislander service, which operates conventional car ferries providing all the services that the catamarans do, but have an upper deck. Here one can stroll and enjoy the fresh sea air and contemplate the passing coastline and the sea in all its glory with its marine life and other vessels which travel on its surface. How often I wondered, as I surveyed my fellow passengers filling their mouths with cakes and coke, have they seen this coastline and its marine life? Perhaps it wasn't important, but cakes and coke come everyday and everywhere and what I was trying to watch from the cramped deck at the stern was for me a once in a lifetime sight.

Cook Strait can be one of New Zealand's nastiest stretches of water and quite often visibility is marred by fog or just plain heavy rain and low cloud. We were lucky, it was a lovely sunny day with a light wind and not a cloud in the sky as we set off towards the narrow entrance at the end of this great natural harbour. Soon we were heading out into the open sea with Baring Head on our port hand. Baring Head has the distinction of being surmounted by the oldest lighthouse in the country. It was erected in 1859 and has since been joined by a comparative youngster, which knows its place in the pecking order and stands respectfully at the foot of the knoll almost on the waterline, where it can be seen when its older and loftier relative is hidden in low cloud.

We turned and sailed past Sinclair Head, where the grey fur seals make their home in winter, before heading across the strait to the Tory Channel which would take us into Queen Charlotte Sound.

Over two hundred years ago in January 1770, Captain Cook in HMS Endeavour was also in these waters. He had sailed around the North Island from the Bay of Poverty on the east coast up past Cape Reinga and down the west coast. He had just sighted a high mountain "very much like the Peak of Tenerife" with "some very remarkable peaked islands" lying offshore. This was Mount Egmont, a magnificent conical mountain 8,260 feet high, which is surrounded on three sides by the sea and has three baby mountains which pierce the sea and are known as the Sugar-loaf Islands. To the south of this he reported that the land curved away to the south east into what he thought was a great bay. He was looking for somewhere safe to careen the Endeavour, that is to lay the ship on her side, so that the bottom could be scraped of all growth and the seams between the planks caulked to stem the leaks. There were other defects too and the ship needed fresh water, wood for the galley and any fresh vegetables, fish and meat that could be found. In his log for Monday 15th January 1770 he tells how they had sighted an inlet, which he later named Queen Charlotte's Sound. There was hardly any wind and the tide began to sweep him onto the rocky shore and disaster seemed to be upon them. But they lowered all their boats and by the sheer brute force of the sailors at their oars, succeeded in towing the ship clear. With the boats still towing they made their way into a "very snug cove" which is now named Endeavour Inlet.

As soon as they were anchored several native canoes appeared and stones were thrown at them, but with the aid of Tupia the natives were persuaded to venture on board and contact was made. Endeavour was in the inlet for about three weeks and during this time Cook and his crew got to know the local Maoris fairly well. He tells of his horror when he first realised that the Maoris were in fact cannibals, as he had long suspected. On only the second day of his visit they found "a woman floating upon the water, who to all appearance had not been dead many days". Shortly after, they landed and met some natives "who not long before must have been regaling themselves upon human flesh, for I got from one of them the bone of the forearm of a man or woman which was quite fresh". Through Tupia they told them that they had "taken, kill'd and eat a boat's crew of their enemies" and from what they could learn the woman they had seen floating in the water had been in this canoe and had drowned in the fighting. Later, to show Cook, one of the natives "bit and naw'd the bone and draw'd it through his mouth in such a manner as plainly shew'd that the flesh to him was a dainty bit".

The next day some of his men found three hip-bones of men. "They lay near a hole or oven, that is a place where the natives dress their victuals". The Maori oven, usually known as an umu, was a hole in the ground. A great fire was lit in the umu, by which stones were heated. The hot stones were covered with leaves, the food placed on top and then more leaves were laid on. Finally water was sprinkled over and earth spread over the contents and stamped down hard. The imprisoned steam then cooked the food. This method is still used in the Fiji Islands, mainly for the benefit of tourists.

A day or so later the natives brought four of the heads of the men killed in the fighting. The Maoris were experts in the preservation of heads, both of their enemies and friends, the former as an act of revenge and the latter an act of piety and affection. Once good relations had been established with the Maoris in the early nineteenth century, a brisk trade developed in the sale of these awful objects. In 1831, a chief went aboard a trading vessel and there saw the heads of a number of his friends, which were destined for the cabinets of curio-hunters. Greatly distressed, the chief went to see his friend the Reverend Samuel Marsden, who took the matter up with Governor Darling and a Proclamation was issued prohibiting the trade.

On a more tranquil note the young botanist in the crew, later to become Sir Joseph Banks, wrote of the time spent in Endeavour Inlet, "I was awakened by the singing of the birds ashore, from whence we are distant not a quarter of a mile. They seemed to strain their throats and made, perhaps, the most melodious music I have ever heard, almost emulating small bells, but with the most tunable silver sound imaginable." Was he hearing the lovely fluid song of the bellbird?

On 23rd January Captain Cook took a crewman with him and climbed to the top of one of the hills and reported, "I was abundantly recompensed for the trouble I had in ascending the hill, for from it I saw what I took to be the Eastern Sea and a Strait or passage to it from the Western Sea". On the 6th February 1770 Endeavour weighed anchor and set off eastwards to make the passage of the strait. The same strait which we were crossing in the Lynx. Now it is called Cook Strait and his passage was the start of his voyage round the South Island, which completed the first circumnavigation and charting of New Zealand.

We on the Lynx, however, had a more humble aim – that of getting to Picton. The Tory channel is narrow and fiord-like and at its southern entrance stands a group of rocky little islands, which I suspect in poor visibility have been the cause of many a mariner's shipwreck. But with the sun shining on them and the glistening calm sea gently breaking on their shores they looked benign and welcoming. Our crossing ended with a beautiful trip through Charlotte Sound with its tree-covered hills and sheltered coves, and finally we were at Picton, where a new land waited patiently for us to explore.

Chapter Eleven

WETLAND

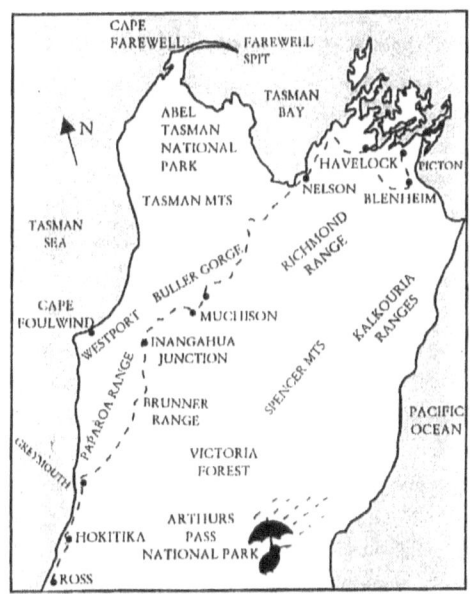

WEST COAST

If you want to holiday in the Marlborough Sounds Maritime Park, which embraces all the fjords that divide this tip of the South Island into a myriad of islands and peninsulas, then Picton must be your start point. There are a number of cruises in and around the bays, to say nothing of the many opportunities for walking, including a four-day twenty-eight-mile guided walk, during which, the brochure says, "your pack will be carried for you and meals and accommodation provided". At seven miles a day with no pack, no wonder it's "suitable for the fit seventies"!

Apart from tourism, which doesn't seem to have taken over the area in quite the same way as it has in others, Picton exists mainly for the ferries and is the railhead for the mainline railway in the South Island. Judging by the boats in the harbour, there is also a large fishing community and it must also be a wonderful area in which to simply mess about in a boat!

I had read somewhere about an old East Indiaman, which had been rescued from the breakers yard and was now lying in Picton and I was keen to see this piece of maritime history. And there just by the ferry terminal was the Edwin Fox museum, named after this old ship. It was certainly something I would have been sad to have missed. Only the vandalised hull remains, but its story is told in this excellent museum. She started life on the slipways at Sulkeah in Bengal, where she was to be the last of many ships built there for the Honourable East India Company, which effectively ruled India. These ships, which had to withstand the long voyages in all weathers from India to England round the Cape of Good Hope, were built of massive baulks of timber. In England oak was used, but in India teak and saul were the hard woods, which gave the hull its immense strength.

Edwin Fox, named after an official in the East India Company, only completed one voyage as an East Indiaman, before she was chartered to the British Government for use as a troop transport in the Crimean War. When the war was over she paid the first of many visits to the Antipodes, when she was again chartered by the British Government to transport convicts to Fremantle, Western Australia. Two hundred and eighty convicts found guilty of political crimes made the voyage, caged like animals for a terrible passage lasting nearly thirteen whole weeks. But this was the only time she carried convicts.

Later she made several voyages carrying immigrants to New Zealand and had several near disasters. Once after a gale in the English Channel she sprang a leak and with her sails in shreds and partially dismasted she hoisted a lady's red petticoat as a distress signal. Her passengers were rescued by the American steamer "Copernicus", who then towed Edwin Fox to Brest for repairs. On another occasion she collided with a schooner and was stranded on the sands off Deal. Such were the perils that these intrepid immigrants suffered in their quest for a new life!

She spent her last few voyages carrying cargo between England Australia and New Zealand until eventually sail had to give way to steam. But the old ship still had a useful life for in 1885 her decks were cleared, her masts shortened and coal-fired boilers were installed to provide steam to drive the refrigeration machinery installed on her deck to freeze the sheep meat from the South Island farms. Then in 1905 a shore-side refrigeration plant was built and the Edwin Fox was mutilated. Large holes were cut in her sides and many of her bulkheads removed and she became a landing stage and a coal hulk for the plant ashore. Finally in the 1950s for some unknown reason her decks were removed. This final act of vandalism reduced her to her present sorry state. But this tough old veteran resisted her attackers to the end and in so doing bent many of the crowbars being used to prise her apart.

Now the people of Picton are conscious of the loss of this relic of the past and there are valiant hopes that one day she may be restored. In the meantime the museum reminds us of how she was built and how she sailed the world and gathers a little money for the enormous effort of restoring her, as a view of the hulk emphasises.

The state of this once proud ship made me feel sad and despondent. But then I realised that despite everything man had done to her, she still resolutely refused to sink and I thought of the nameless Bengalis who had shaped and joined those huge timbers to make her come alive. They could feel proud of their work which has spanned the centuries. I wish the Preservation Society well.

We left Picton and set off for Blenheim, well known for its viniculture. Montana Wines seems to be the biggest vineyard around and produce both red and white wines, which we enjoyed throughout our travels in the South Island.

We were aiming to drive down the west coast to see the Franz Josef and the Fox glaciers, so at Blenheim we turned westwards and then after a few miles we branched off to the north to visit Nelson.

The drive took us through Havelock, a little port standing where the Pelorus river flows into the southern end of the Marlborough Sounds. Now it is given over to fishing, but in its heyday it served the brief life of the Wakamarina goldfield. Along the Rai river valley we drove and then after climbing over the Bryant Range of timber-clad hills we approached Nelson.

Nelson is situated at the southern end of Tasman Bay and it is near here that the Dutch navigator Abel Tasman anchored some two hundred and fifty years ago in 1642, and had that unfriendly encounter with the local Maoris, resulting in the death of four of his crew. He named the bay in which he had anchored Murderers Bay and left. Today its called Golden Bay and forms part of the Abel Tasman National Park dominated by Mount Evans, which rises 3,500 feet above sea level.

In 1838 the New Zealand Company, founded to bring settlers from Britain, bought land in the area in order to establish a settlement to be named Nelson. The land was then subdivided back in England and sold 'sight unseen' to families of hopeful immigrants. The advance party of the settlers arrived in the sailing ship Arrow and set to work clearing land and felling trees, and eagerly awaited the arrival of their wives and children sailing in a later ship. But when the vessel finally arrived all the women were suffering from scurvy after a voyage which had lasted five months. But the real tragedy was an epidemic of whooping-cough, which had broken out on the ship and had killed fifty-eight of the children.

What made these immigrants willing to suffer the terrible dangers and risks associated with these long and unpredictable sea voyages? Either the lot of the poor in Victorian England must have been so desperate and their prospects so bleak, or the promise of a brighter and more prosperous life so persuasive. Perhaps they just didn't know what trials and tribulations they had to face. No doubt their enthusiasm carried them through the farewells, the embarkation and the early stages of the passage. But what inner strengths they needed to survive the journey and to arrive in a strange new land, where nothing could be certain! From the viewpoint of our cosseted twentieth century life it seems unbelievable that so many people would embark on such an unpredictable, dangerous and risky venture.

But despite the ordeal and wretchedness of these early immigrant passages, three thousand more settlers had arrived during the next three or four years. The settlement grew and was named after Admiral Lord Nelson. The Battle of Trafalgar, together with the Admirals and Captains who fought with him, are remembered in the street names of the town. Today Nelson has a population of forty-eight thousand and is a popular holiday area with fine beaches and bays close at hand and plenty of sunshine and is the centre of a large and successful fruit-growing industry.

To get to the west coast we now had to cross the Brunner Range and to do so the road follows the Buller River, which over the centuries has carved its winding route through precipitous gorges and steep valleys, to which primeval ferns, cabbage trees and ancient timber cling in wild profusion. As we drove the weather began to break and low clouds obscured the mountain tops. We became enclosed by these dark brooding mountains on this empty winding road and our feeling of loneliness grew, so we were thankful that we seemed to have a reliable car to carry us on our journey.

We had recently seen an incredible picture of the South Island, taken from outer space, which showed with unbelievable clarity the fault line running straight as an arrow the length of the island. The fault line is the junction of two plates in the earth's crust, which are slowly sliding past each other causing stresses, often resulting in earthquakes. The Buller Gorge follows this fault line and subsidence and landslides have caused many changes in the gorge. In 1929 an earthquake centred on Murchison lifted the land in its vicinity about twelve feet and further on at Inangahua Junction, where the Inangahua River joins the Buller, an earthquake in 1968 measuring over seven on the Richter scale blocked the river and the scarred hillsides can still be seen.

Past Inangahua Junction the gorge becomes very narrow. When in f lood the river here can rise over eighty feet in a few hours and the local hotel at Berlins has some interesting tales to tell of past f loods. This part of the gorge is very beautiful, with the azure-coloured river tumbling and racing between sheer cliffs overhung by tenacious willows and native bush. At Hawk's Crag the gorge is so narrow that a single lane road in a kind of tunnel with an open side overlooking the river has been blasted out of the overhanging cliffs. As we drove through water flowed in small streams down the rock face to join the Buller just below us and we felt that wet suits might shortly be needed! Indeed at the peak of the worst floods ever in 1926, the level of the river was several feet above the top of the arch!

Once through Hawk's Crag life took on a more normal aspect and soon we were clear of the forest and driving along the coast with a stiff breeze blowing in from Cape Foulwind, as the land which juts out into the Tasman Sea is called. Now, instead of a tumbling river to keep us company, we had a grey sea endlessly attacking the flotsam-strewn beaches with crested rollers driven by an onshore wind. Inshore the bush-covered hills climbed up into the mist and we saw the first spots of rain on the windscreen. We also saw that our petrol was running low and realised that we hadn't seen a petrol station since leaving Nelson that morning. I found it difficult to enjoy the scenery and began to economise on fuel consumption by freewheeling down the hills. The road was still practically deserted, and hitching a lift to a distant garage for petrol and hitching back again was not a very encouraging prospect. By now we had a little red light flashing on the petrol gauge to add to our sense of urgency and still no sign of fuel!

Greymouth was still about ten miles away and our fears were growing, when we approached Runanga and there thankfully we saw a petrol station. It was about 1.30 in the afternoon as we drew in and the first thing we saw was a notice saying "Sorry no petrol until 3pm"! There had been a power cut, but our luck was in, it had just been restored and once again we had a full tank. On travels such as this we never let the petrol fall below half and had set off that morning with three quarters of a tank. It had been a long run without petrol stations and though we aimed in future to refill at the three-quarter point, we never again experienced such a long gap between garages.

Through Greymouth we drove and then onto Hokitika across two very unusual bridges. Often the bridges are one way only and one direction has right of way, and by now we had got used to these, but then one after another we met these two bridges. Again they were one way, but running down the centre of the narrow roadway was the narrow gauge New Zealand railway line! "Give way to Trains", said the notice, but what happens if you meet a speeding train halfway across? We crossed with trepidation, but talking about this to some locals later I was assured the train approaches slowly and only crosses when the way ahead is clear.

The discovery of gold at Greenstone Creek near Hokitika started a rush to the West Coast. In November 1864 the town consisted of a calico store on one side of the river and four stores on the other with a few tents erected by the prospectors. Within a year or two this hastily established community had grown into a more permanent township with a population of some six thousand with about one hundred hotels and grog shanties. It had become the fourth busiest port in the country and on one occasion sixty ships were moored, many four abreast, in the little harbour in the mouth of the Hokitika river. So cramped was the anchorage with its entry constrained by a dangerous sand bar, that at the height of the rush on average one ship was damaged in collision or wrecked on the bar every ten days. Despite these hazards, in the first twelve years of the rush nearly three and a half million ounces of gold were exported through the little port. Nowadays the rush is over and the port is neglected, and such seaborne trade as there is uses Greymouth to the north.

Gold is an extremely heavy metal and has a resplendent lustre which doesn't tarnish. Because of its brilliant appearance and occurrence naturally in river mud, it was almost certainly the first metal to attract the attention of man. It was known and highly valued by the earliest civilisations, such as the Egyptian and Minoan, and from such periods ornaments of great variety and beautiful and elaborate workmanship have survived. Just think of that golden head of Tutankhamun in his tomb. But it couldn't be used even for ornaments until the art of smelting had been perfected in the bronze age. The earliest mining is thought to have taken place in Egypt and gold washing is depicted on monuments dating back to 2900 BC. The legend of the Golden Fleece describes how Jason set sail in a galley with his band of Argonauts in the thirteenth century BC in search of the fleece on a journey which took them from Greece to ancient Colchis in the state of Georgia in the former Soviet Union. It was there that Jason found not only the Golden Fleece, but also his bride Medea, after taming the wild bulls and killing the serpent. But what was the fleece? Well, the locals were using sheepskins to sift out the gold from the river sands and when successful the fleece became covered with gold.

Gold is often found in minute particles in river sand and gravels, especially where the river flows through crystalline rocks. To extract the gold particles the mud and sand are swirled around in a shallow pan. The heavier gold settles to the bottom and the mud and sand are gradually washed away by dipping the pan into the water and pouring it off. From this the miner's cradle was developed, so called because it resembled a child's rocking cradle. At the top is a box with a perforated bottom into which sand and gravel are shovelled and water is poured in. The action of the water and the rocking motion allow the finer gravel to fall through into an inclined trough below, where the liquid mud flows over little strips of wood set at right angles to the flow. These strips or 'riffles' retard the heavier element, i.e. the gold, while the rest flows to the end of the trough. The detritus trapped by the riffles was finally panned to extract the gold.

The idea of the cradle was developed further and huge sluice boxes perhaps one hundred yards long were erected with riffles at regular intervals. These sluice boxes were then fed with mud and gravel by means of powerful jets of water driven by a head of water sometimes as high as two hundred feet. The need for great quantities of water at high pressure thus became paramount and in 1866 the Totara Water Race Company raised £1,360 of local capital and laboured for ten months on a six-mile race to bring water to the area. Eighty thousand feet of timber was used in the building of the flumes, an aqueduct 573 feet long and 130 feet high was made, and eighteen tunnels were also dug.

By 1867 in Ross a little way south of Hokitika, shafts were being sunk in Jones' flat to follow the veins. At first men were able to work the shallow bottoms by means of hand windlasses, but once below about forty feet something more powerful than hand-winding gear was needed and a wooden drum or capstan drawn by a horse walking in a circle was used. The "whip" was also developed. This was a stout pole set at an angle of about 45 degrees over the mouth of the shaft with a pulley at the end. A bullock-hide bucket in the shaft was connected by a rope led through the pulley to a horse which walked up and down a prepared track, thus raising and lowering the bucket.

Many shafts were sunk and a reporter visiting the area in February 1866 declared that "during a half mile walk on Jones' Flat" he could see "as many holes in the ground as in a nutmeg grater". Here on the West Coast it is notoriously wet and it rains for about two hundred days in the year; and it is not for nothing that Westland is known to the locals as Wetland. In these terrible conditions the gold diggers worked their shafts twenty-four hours a day, otherwise when they started work in the morning much time was wasted just pumping the shaft dry. The work was hard and constant and the deep shafts, lined from top to bottom with wood to prevent falls, were considerable engineering feats.

Though the men worked in these abysmal conditions, with long hours, inadequate shelter and poor food, records from the period show that some parties were getting a return from their labours of between £20 and £30 per man per week and the average seems to have been about £14. Such returns in the 1870s were enormous. What would £25 in 1870 be worth in 1990? Twenty times as much? Possibly more, but even at twenty times that would equate to £500 per week of our money or £25,000 a year. Without tax that was big money! No wonder men followed the call of the gold.

Today gold is still worked in a few places in New Zealand, but not on a regular basis in the Hokitika area. In slack periods some builders and construction companies work a local shaft or two but nowadays with the economy thriving they are busy with their normal work.

At Shantytown just up the road there is a faithful recreation of the old West Coast mining town complete with hotel, shops and even a church. There is a Chinese den, jail with its gallows and a working gold claim where one can try one's hand at panning. It gives one a very vivid picture of life during the height of the rush. Incidentally the largest golden nugget ever mined in New Zealand was found in Ross by a digger called "the Honourable Roddy" in 1909. Of massive size it weighed 99 ounces 12 pennyweight.

The rain was now coming down like the proverbial stair rods as we approached Ferguson, where we had planned to stay at a local farm. I thought we would get drowned just getting out of the car and unloading our bags. But the locals know all about rain in these parts and a nice dry car port just outside the front door welcomed us.

Our hosts were third-generation Kiwis. His grandfather, who was Irish originally, went to Australia. I didn't feel I could ask whether his emigration to Australia was voluntary or not, but in 1870 he came to New Zealand and landed in Hokitika to take part in the great rush for gold. He must have made a bit of capital and his son, our host's father, built and ran a small hotel south of Ross. While the gold was still being worked the hotel was profitable and he bought land to farm. In the 1940s the hotel was pulled down and the farm extended. His son, now in his seventies, runs the three-and-a-half-thousand acre farm with one permanent worker and occasional part-time help. He farms mainly for beef, with a herd of Herefords, that lovely stocky red breed with short straight horns above a big white head, and also rears blackfaced Suffolk sheep for meat and wool.

His land is in four parcels and he, his wife and his farm hand are all on walkie talkies, and while we were having our introductory cup of tea we could hear the chatter on the receiver in the kitchen. Their son had attended the Agriculture College at Lincoln, near Christchurch, and also at Massey, not far from Wellington in the North Island. Now he is working as a researcher at Lincoln. Meanwhile father is thinking of retirement and hoping their son will take over so that he and his wife can move nearer to the east coast to have a few last years in the dry! Their bungalow was quite spacious and had been built in the fifties with lots of lovely amber-coloured rimu wood for doors, windows and fittings.

Staying at farms like this is a wonderful way to get to know the Kiwis and to hear all about the local history and their view of the world. Our visit was only marred by the constant rain, which prevented us from looking around the farm. But one framed poem in the hall said it all:

Dick Parsons

It rained and rained and rained
The average fall was well maintained
And when the tracks were simply
bogs It started raining cats and dogs.

After a drought of half an hour
We had a most refreshing shower
And then the most curious thing of all
A gentle rain began to fall.

Next day also was fairly dry
Save for a deluge from the sky
Which wetted the party to the skin
And after that the rain set in.

Chapter Twelve
LAND OF GLACIERS

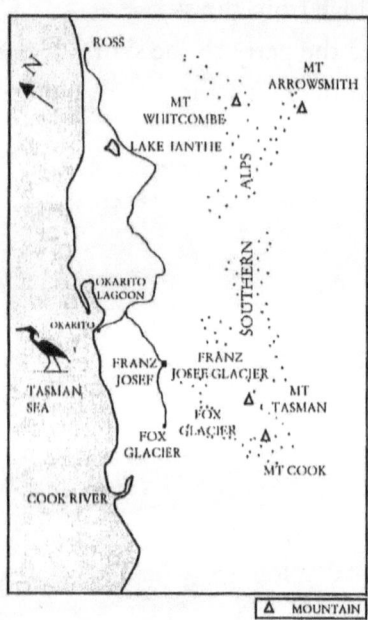

The next morning the rain stopped, but low clouds were hovering overhead, everything was saturated and after saying goodbye to our new friends we set off in a scotch mist. The road is a very well-maintained single carriageway cut through lowland rain forest with occasional breaks for farms, lakes and views of the grey restless Tasman sea on our right. One crosses innumerable bridges over rivers and creeks, the rivers usually having Maori sounding names but the creeks, which in

UK we would call streams or even torrents, are often named after the local farmer. Thus you might have Paddy's Creek and if there is more than one creek on Paddy's land then you might have Paddy's Creek N° 1 and N° 2 and so on. It's quite a novel way of naming the creeks but essentially quite practical and avoids all the intellectual effort of thinking of appropriate names!

We had just settled into our drive when the road skirted Lake Ianthe. How this lake acquired the name of the bride of Duke Alphonso of Sicily is not clear, but on this misty still morning it was quite beautiful with its forest-fringed shores and tranquil surface. With so little traffic on the road we enjoyed the peace and quiet.

Our experience of the rain the previous day helped us to understand that here we were driving through real live rain forest. The trees are all covered with mosses and lichens and the forest floor has a multitude of differing ferns. The dominant trees are podocarps which, as far as a layman like me understands, is a conifer tree which has small rather spindly cones, unlike our more usual fir trees with their conical shaped ones. But their most important characteristic is that they take their sustenance from water and sunlight and therefore can grow on solid rock.

The rarest is the spindly kahikatea or white pine, New Zealand's tallest tree which can reach a height of about 180 feet. The great length of its trunk made it a favourite timber of the Maoris for their canoes. Its wood is very light in colour and weight and was at one time used to make butter and cheese boxes. It has green scale-like leaves and little yellow cones and produces a reddish oval berry with a seed stuck on top, which used to be gathered by the Maoris as they enjoyed its sweet taste. The berry was also a favourite food of the native pigeons, which the Maoris learnt to snare on the trees.

Other trees such as the totara, which lives for 1,000 years or more and the matai or black pine which has a thick dark grey bark that flakes off revealing distinctive scarlet patches beneath, also inhabit the rain forest. But by far the easiest tree to recognise is the rimu, the red pine. It grows to a height of 160 feet or thereabouts and has a greyish brown flaky bark. The narrow overlapping spine-like leaves hang down in graceful festoons with tiny ripe red cones appearing on the tips of the leaves in season. Charcoal made from rimu was mixed with grease by the Maoris to rub into tattoo incisions to make the indelible markings. It's a lovely tree and once you have recognised it you will start to see it all over the place.

On the Waitangiroto River, north of Okarito Lagoon, there is a small breeding colony of white herons, which we would have loved to see. But sadly access is restricted to those people who can produce evidence that they are genuine ornithologists. However the lagoon, one of the largest wetlands in New Zealand, consisting of shallow open water and tidal f lats, is a feeding ground for all kinds of waders and water-fowl, including the white heron and the royal spoonbill. We turned off at The Forks and took the little unmetalled road to Okarito on the coast at the southern end of the lagoon and there, as we had hoped, was a solitary white heron feeding in the shallows. What a thrill that was, but what a pity we didn't see a spoonbill!

Okarito in its prime was another gold mining town, but apart from an old miner's cradle mounted on wheels lying derelict in the long grass and the jetty at the mouth of the lagoon nothing remained to tell of the time when over ten thousand miners were panning in the area for alluvial gold. Now a few empty holiday cottages surround the obelisk erected in 1940 to commemorate Tasman's landfall on this coast in December 1642 and Captain Cook's passage in March 1770.

We walked down to the beach which stretched away to the south, where the Tasman Sea was as busy as ever propelling its surf towards the shoreline in its never-ending onslaught of the land. The beach was made up of a fine blue grey sand, which was littered with the remains of trees stripped of their bark and whitened by the elements, and just above the waterline a long stretch of spume shivered and wobbled in the wind, in which the gulls soared. We enjoyed the spectacle and then the loneliness of the place got to us and we headed back to the shelter of the land.

As we strolled around this old gold mining settlement, I thought how ironic it was that gold should have been discovered at Greenstone Creek! Greenstone was important to the Maoris as a source of wealth and for the manufacture of cutting tools. So important, in fact, that the various tribes would fight over it if need be. But as the Maoris were literally stone age people they knew nothing of the art of smelting metal, so the little nuggets of gold they might have discovered were of no importance to them. Likewise their prized greenstone, which presumably could have been found in Greenstone Creek, was of little importance to the European miners, but they in turn would fight over the shiny yellow dust!

The fault line, which we had encountered in the Buller Gorge, is the real culprit for all the rain which the West Coast experiences. The collision of the two Earth's Crustal plates, the Indo-Australian and the Pacific, has formed this fault in the earth's surface, which stretches in this incredibly straight line nearly four hundred miles along the western edge of the Southern Alps from Milford Sound in the south to Nelson in the north. Massive movements along this fault line over many millions of years have pushed the Pacific plate sixty to seventy thousand feet up over the Indo-Australian plate and given birth to the Southern Alps. The presence of limestone layers containing shell fossils at the top of some of the southern mountains confirms this and shows that at some time they must have been below sea level. Now the Southern Alps present an obstacle to the moist westerly winds of the roaring forties and, as they hit the slopes of the mountains, the moist air is forced to rise. As it rises it cools, clouds form and then it starts to rain and the lowland rain forests of the West Coast get about fifteen feet of rain in a year, while on the eastern side of the Alps the air has lost its moisture and gains temperature as it descends and f lows over the plains as a hot dry wind.

In winter the rain falls as snow and on the mountains it can snow at any time, and here the annual precipitation can reach an unbelievable fifty feet! The snow compresses and forms ice, which under gravity starts to creep downhill from the high mountain snow fields in an "ice river". There are about one hundred and forty glaciers in this part of New Zealand, but the most well known are Fox and Franz Josef glaciers.

During the ice ages of the last two million years glaciers and snowfalls smothered much of the mountains and lowlands, and the

Fox and Franz Josef are just the shrunken remnants of their former selves! Great glaciers of up to forty five thousand feet thick repeatedly advanced and retreated along the gaps between mountains scouring out their great U-shaped valleys and dumping vast quantities of moraine on to the plains below. Moraine is the name given to the rocks and other rubble eroded from the mountains by the glacier as it grinds its way through the narrow valleys.

In these great ice ages sea levels were about three hundred feet lower than they are now and both the Fox and Franz Josef flowed well beyond the present coastline. But about 14,000 years ago temperatures began to rise and the ice retreated. Vast forests now began to regain a hold on the land and today forested moraines can be seen in the lowlands marking the routes the glaciers once took on their journey to the sea. Meanwhile glacial water filled many of the depressions scraped out by the ice, forming the myriad of lakes we see today.

Franz Joseph Glacier was only discovered in 1862 and Julius Von Haast named it after the Emperor of Austria-Hungary. It flows for eight miles during which it falls about eight thousand feet and ends in an abrupt ice cliff about nine hundred yards wide and one hundred feet high. A sediment laden-grey torrent, which becomes the Waiho River, emerges from the glacier snout looking like a tunnel at the base of this great ice cliff. Large chunks of ice flow in the river like mini-icebergs and as the warm air meets this icy stream it condenses giving off clouds of steam.

As we approached the settlement at Franz Joseph it began to rain again and the low clouds made it quite plain that there was no chance of seeing either Mount Cook or Mount Tasman, but nevertheless we made our way up to the lookout and saw the glacier with its huge wall of blue white ice sliding down the valley and terminating in this steamy grey river. Until recently one could walk to the glacier snout along the river bank, but the path had been washed away and hadn't been restored when we were there. So we had to view the glacier from a distance. Seeing this massive crevassed wall of ice coming down from the grey clouds above us and squeezing itself between the dark near vertical walls of the valley was an unforgettable sight.

A few miles further south we drove into the little village of Fox Glacier, where we booked into the Fox Glacier Hotel, which is the oldest in town and has been run since it first opened by three generations of the same family. Built at the turn of the century, its old coal-fired range now forms a centrepiece in the main lounge, where a lovely log fire burned in the fireplace. The kitchens have been rehoused, additional single-storey wings have pushed out from the main block, and life in the town seems to revolve around the hotel, which also acts as the wine shop, pub and long-distance bus stop.

The Fox Glacier was first called the Albert Glacier after Queen Victoria's consort, but it is now named after the former Prime Minister of New Zealand, William Fox, who was an artist of note and visited and painted here in the 1870s. It is a bit longer than Franz Josef, being nearly nine miles long, and falls almost ten thousand feet. But its path is not so steep as Franz Joseph, which moves at a greater speed varying from one to five yards a day depending on the season.

That evening and again the next day we went to look at the Fox Glacier, that rises in the snow fields of Mount Tasman, which understudies Mount Cook as the highest in the Alps. However, the low cloud persisted and the intermittent rain did nothing to improve the visibility. First we drove up the Glacier Access road, which starts a couple of miles south of the village. The road skirts the turbulent glacial waters of the Cook river and rises through the forested moraines to a car park to give one a closer view of the terminal. But again we were out of luck as a rock fall had blocked the road and we couldn't get far and really couldn't see the glacier.

Disappointed, we returned to the hotel to study the maps and literature we had and discovered that across the Cook River, there is another track leading up towards the glacier. The next day, we followed this road, but again a notice told us we could go no further. We did find a vantage point and were able to see this giant of a glacier coming down between the bare rock with a dog-leg part way down before its terminal. From our viewpoint we looked down on the glacier so we were able to see a lot of its course and even in the gloom we could see the lovely pale blue of the ice wall.

One can get a light plane and fly over the glaciers, even landing on them for a quick game of snowballs. There are also helicopters which fly you up the mountains, but you need fine weather and good visibility for such trips which are part of modern tourism. But in the weather we experienced we had to be content with our meagre glimpses, though I think in an odd sort of way, the sight of these great works of nature shrouded in mist adds to their mystery and emphasises the great power they have, which they have exercised almost since time began.

Chapter Thirteen

HAAST AND BEYOND

The morning we left Fox, the rain had stopped, though the low clouds threatened to renew the onslaught, so with great expectations of sun on the other side of the mountains we set off down the coast road to cross the Alps via the Haast Pass.

The West Coast, which stretches about one hundred and fifty miles from Greyport to the tiny township of Haast, only has a population of about 30,000 and must be one of the rare unspoilt areas of the world, where rain forest, glaciers and mountains reign supreme and man so far has made little impact. Unfortunately, that great polluter, tourism, is now at work, but who am I to complain as a tourist myself? However let us hope that this vital industry, which has brought employment and prosperity to the locals can be developed sensibly, as it has to date, without despoiling this beautiful area.

After driving for about three hours through forests and alongside lakes and finally the sea itself we arrived at Haast, a handful of houses with a petrol station and an excellent visitors' centre full of pamphlets and with a very good display of the geography and history of the area.

For more than a century the little township was the end of the road. There was and there still is no road further down the coast and a road over the mountains to link the West Coast with Wanaka and the East Coast had always been an elusive dream for those who lived in the isolated settlements of the West Coast south of Fox. The Maoris used a route from the East, which took them over the mountains in their quest for greenstone, but it was a long and hazardous journey not to be made too often. The first European to find a pass over the mountains was a gold prospector named Charles Cameron who trekked across country from Dunedin in 1863. Not far behind him was Julius von Haast and somehow the pass was named after him! What a pity, I think Cameron Pass sounds better than Haast Pass, but anyway Haast got the glory and of course it was he who also named the Franz Josef Glacier.

Some fifteen years later the pass was being used regularly as a packhorse trail but it wasn't until 1929 that work began at the eastern end to build a proper road from Waneka. In 1939 work started at the West Coast end with the aim of meeting half way, but soon ceased with the onset of World War II. In 1956 work began again, this time with more modern equipment and finally Highway 6, which climbs over the pass, was opened in 1965. With interruptions for the war, the work had taken thirty-six years and had required the building of numerous bridges in an area prone to flooding, ice and snow. The bridge over the Haast River is enormous and like most in this area is single lane. It had to be built ten feet above the highest known flood level and is 800 yards long. It is New Zealand's longest bridge.

For the first twenty-odd miles we followed the Haast River and climbed through the Makaketake forest with the intriguingly named mountain Shattered Peak on our left. I thought of our young, who so frequently throw themselves into a chair with those time-honoured words 'I'm shattered' and wondered what this poor mountain had done to acquire this name! Once abreast this poor shattered peak, the road veered off to the right and soon we were approaching the Gates of Haast and then the summit of the pass itself at 1,850 feet. Now we had Mount Aspiring National Park on our right, a wild and rugged area, whose centrepiece Mount Aspiring rises in a classical pyramid shape to nearly ten thousand feet piercing its encircling glaciers. For the energetic and adventurous young this is a great area for trekking and climbing, where chamois and red deer can be seen.

As we broke out of the surrounding hills we met the Makarora River and for the first time in ages, or so it seemed, the sun shone and all the beautiful colours of the surrounding mountains and the river itself came alive. Our road followed the river until it flowed into Lake Wanaka filled with glacial water, which is a lovely turquoise blue, a colour one takes for granted after a while, but on first sight it's almost breathtaking. Then, after following the shores of Lake Wanaka for ten miles or so, the road switched its loyalty to Lake Hawea to the east and then after a few more miles we cut inshore and drove into Waneka itself standing at the southern end of the lake. With the sun shining out of a cloudless sky and the lovely blue water of the lake glistening in the rays of the sun, we felt immersed in the holiday atmosphere which imbues this little lakeside settlement.

We had arranged to stay at a homestay and soon found our new hosts house a little way from the lake, but with lovely views of the mountains. Our hosts were retired farmers, whose son now runs their farm up on the high land of the Remarkables, where they have some eleven thousand sheep and two hundred head of beef cattle. He told me that his great-grandfather had been a cadet in the Merchant Navy, but when he heard about the goldrush in New Zealand he jumped ship to go after the gold. But then, perhaps because he wasn't having much luck in the search for gold or perhaps because he saw the opportunity, he decided that supplying goods for the gold diggers was more profitable than digging for gold. And so it was and soon he had four stores selling to the diggers, which he ran with the help of his sons, who took over the business when he died. But while our host's grandfather ran the stores, his father bought land and started the family farm, now being run by their son. Though farming on these high country farms is lonely with demanding physical work, it is obviously profitable as our hosts had a very comfortable house with a lovely garden and had travelled widely in Europe and the States.

Just outside Wanaka on the road to Cromwell is the New Zealand Fighter Pilots Museum. This records the heroism of many Kiwi airmen of World War II and also has on display many fighters of World Wars I and II. Planes like the SE5A, Kittyhawk, Mustang, Corsair and of course the unforgettable Spitfire of Battle of Britain fame. New Zealand made a tremendous contribution to the air effort in the 1939-45 war out of all proportion to her population. New Zealanders flew with great success not only in Fighters but also in Bombers. Eighty-seven NZ pilots became 'fighter aces', an accolade given to those who were particularly successful in shooting down enemy aircraft. The Corsair was a naval aircraft, which f lew from the many carriers the Royal Navy operated during the war and here again the Kiwis made a large contribution. The Kiwis have always had an expertise in f lying, brought about by the sparseness of the population in a land of mountains and forests with rugged terrain making the building of roads and railways difficult and costly. While slower ships and boats could exploit the coastal and inland waterways, small planes were able to give speedy and direct communications, and many small towns even before the war had their own airstrips, which nowadays are also used for f lying tourists over the many great natural attractions.

Besides the static display of fighters in the museum are some veteran aircraft still being used, such as the Tiger Moth, a much-loved biplane in which most pilots of World War II learnt to f ly. Another veteran of pre-war days is the de Havilland Domine. This elegant big sister of the Tiger Moth, with its twin engines and be-spatted landing wheels, carries eight passengers, and before the war and for some years afterwards could be seen f lying quietly over England; but regrettably no more. But here in the South Island this survivor of a more gentle age still gives its passengers the thrill of early f lying.

Leaving the museum, we drove along the banks of Lake Dunstan, which was dammed in 1992 to drive yet another hydroelectric generator, thus submerging part of Cromwell, the next town through which we drove. Originally the centre of a gold rush, the town named after Oliver Cromwell, the Protector of England, is now surrounded by fruit farms, and the former miners' water races have long been converted into irrigation channels.

Leaving Cromwell we followed the course of the Kawarau river as it dug its gorge between the Pisa and the Carrick ranges and headed westwards towards Queenstown. The gorge presents some spectacular scenery and at the western end we came across one of New Zealand's newest industries. The Bungy Jump, a Kiwi invention, is definitely for the young and for them it's the 'high' afterwards, and I suppose the certificate, which can only be the attraction. The intrepid adventurers jump from the Kawarau Suspension Bridge, built in the 1880s, which can now only be used by pedestrians and those with a suicidal tendency. The fall from the bridge to the river below, where the jumpers are rescued by dinghy, hopefully without getting wet after bouncing up and down a few times, is 335 feet. That is the equivalent of jumping from the top of a high-rise block of flats of forty storeys! And yet they queue to do it; I suppose the young need a challenge! And a challenge it most certainly is, for don't let anyone delude himself that there's no danger in it, for in the autumn of 1996 it all went terribly wrong for one brave youngster. He had thrown himself off the bridge and the bungy had stopped him and had begun to pull him up as the elastic retracted. Then once more he fell towards that raging torrent below. For a second time the elastic reached the end of its stretch and retracted, pulling him up for another dive at the water. All seemed routine to those watching the fun, but his third descent ended in disaster. Somehow the bungy broke or the lashing round his heels parted, for this time nothing was there to stop his fall. He fell from a great height into the white waters below and was carried downstream by the surging river, while the safety boat followed desperately in his wake. Luckily he was finally rescued and, I understand, is relatively unhurt, but no doubt he is now consulting the legal profession to obtain some compensation for his brush with death.

Luckily we saw nothing like this, as with the other spectators we watched one brave soul take to the bungy. Clearly she had second thoughts about it, but there was no turning back. The younger element of the spectators began to get restless and urged her on with taunts and catcalls until finally she took the plunge. It was, I suppose, a copybook jump, the bungy checked her fall just as we all thought she'd hit the water and then, after having oscillated up and down for maybe a dozen times on the end of that elastic line, she was eased gently into the safety boat. We were pleased to see her safe and drove off hurriedly lest the bug should catch us! A few miles short of Queenstown we left the main road and turned into Arrowtown, another relic of goldmining days. Now its income comes from the tourists, but despite that it still has an old world charm, with its row of little stone cottages and its main street lined with lovely English deciduous trees, a very rare sight in this country, where nearly all the native trees keep their leaves throughout the year. The avenue of trees is reputed to be a very beautiful sight in the autumn, when the leaves turn to gold and then amber before they finally fall.

The museum here is certainly worth a visit and really portrays the life of its inhabitants over the past hundred years or so. There are also plenty of relics of the Chinese community who came here as labourers and, with their capacity for hard work, made a good living and as usual retained their own culture. The shopping further up the road is tourist orientated, but the buildings, though not all original, are very much in keeping with the history of the town. We found it to be a delightful and restful little place.

Leaving Arrowtown we met Lake Wakatipu and drove along its north-eastern arm before entering Queenstown at the centre of the lake, which wriggles like an elongated letter S through the Eyre, Thompson, Richardson and Hector Mountains, with the Remarkables in the near distance just opposite. It has a beautiful setting with the sparkling blue lake contrasting with the colours and shades of the surrounding mountains with their bare rock, forests and pastures. It is a true holiday resort with plenty to do both in winter and summer.

Again time was limited for us but we decided that a visit to the Walter Peak High Country Farm was a must. Farms in the mountains, where land is comparatively cheap, are usually much bigger than those in the more intensely cultivated f latter lowland areas and are known as High Country farms. I suspect that the farmers in these high country farms feel that they are also of a higher order than their lowland compatriots and perhaps they have some justification, since theirs is a much harsher environment and a lonely one at that.

As if to emphasise the lonely aspect of these farms, the only way to get to the Walter Peak farm is to cross the lake and this was how we met the TSS Earnslaw. TSS I wondered? As a mariner I'd heard of SS meaning Steamship, but I'd never heard of TSS. Well, it means Twin Screw Ship! The TSS Earnslaw is a true veteran and was the last of four vessels which sailed up and around this huge lake delivering stores and passengers, many of whom no doubt had four feet and a few had wings. But her trade diminished as the roads and then motor vehicles were developed and it seemed that she would go the same way as her forbears; but a new trade developed and now she carries the two-footed variety on their journey across the lake to the farm.

She is powered by a coal-fired boiler, which produces steam to drive her two triple-expansion engines, which turn the two screws. She was built in sections at Dunedin on the East Coast and transported by rail to Kingston at the southern end of the lake where she was finally assembled. She was launched in 1912 on the same day as the largest ship then afloat, the White Star liner Titanic sank in the Atlantic on her maiden voyage. The Earnslaw is a beautiful little ship about 170 feet long and does a very creditable thirteen knots, and our journey across the lake with views of mountains on all sides was great.

I'm not sure what we were expecting to find when we arrived, perhaps a simple stone house with a barn or two, or a rambling single-storey wooden one, but not the vast sumptuous immaculately decorated bungalow set in beautiful flower-laden gardens reaching down to the lake. I thought it must be a very profitable farm, but later I found that it was no longer the farmhouse, but had been converted and enlarged to be a restaurant where we were to have tea, and where others later that night would come across the water in the good ship Earnslaw to dine and wine. In fact the whole complex of house, barns and the animals we saw were all laid on for the tourists and we never saw the real farm at all. However, we enjoyed seeing the sheep, angora goats and the Highland cattle and of course the red deer. All are descendants of animals introduced mainly from Britain by the settlers, who in their eagerness to exploit the land and make a good living were unaware of the troubles they were unleashing for the future.

The red deer is a good example of the problems these imported animals were to bring. It was first introduced in 1851 near Nelson and over the next seventy-odd years a further 230 were liberated in North and the South Island. In 1905 another species was brought in when President Theodore Roosevelt presented eighteen wapiti deer to the people of New Zealand, which were set free at George Sound. The deer found the habitat just to their liking and without any predators to control them, bred rapidly and the ever-increasing herds did untold damage to grazing and the native flora and soon became a major pest. Shooting parties were organised and paid for each deer's tail they could produce and up to eighty deer a day were killed. When the numbers had been greatly reduced the survivors were hunted by helicopter and after being anaesthetised by shotgun dart were netted and taken to the newly established venison farms, which now make a contribution to the economy. Red deer still remain at large and no doubt continue to breed successfully.

But the greatest problems were caused by the introduction in the mid-1860s of the rabbit as a source of cheap food for the settlers. The old expression "they breed like rabbits" gives a clue to the speed with which the rabbit population exploded. About thirty young can be born in a year to a single doe in litters of between four and six. Gestation takes thirty days and the doe is usually pregnant again within twenty-four hours of giving birth! They eat the grass, clover and any green vegetation. Farmers hate them and, armed with bright lights to dazzle their prey, shoot them by the score at night. In the early 1950s myxomatosis was introduced into the rabbit population, but failed to spread and now farmers use poisoned carrot baits in an attempt to eradicate this pest.

In the 1880s hundreds of weasels, and thousands of stoats and ferrets, which in UK are natural predators of the rabbit were introduced in the firm belief that this would be the answer to the rabbit menace, but without success. The newcomers found that the ground-nesting birds, lizards and other insects were to their liking and they made little impact on the rabbits. Now they in turn are a pest and are blamed for the falling population of many birds, including the almost defenceless national emblem, the Kiwi.

Further troubles were to be caused by the introduction of the opossum in the 1840s which continued until 1920. It is a marsupial and a native of North America and was brought in to be reared for its fur. But many escaped into the wild and are blamed for the destruction of orchards and the indigenous forests. The opossum is also said to carry bovine TB and is therefore a threat to dairy cattle. They are nocturnal animals and the only opossums one sees are those that have been killed by passing traffic on the roads. Incidentally, the fur trade still does well and in 1980 the value of exported possum furs reached nearly £9 million, so perhaps there is an upside to the opossum menace.

Other foreign species have arrived including the Himalayan tahr released in the South Island in 1904; and another goat, the chamois, was presented by the Emperor of Austria-Hungary in 1907, when two male and eight female were released near Mount Cook.

So what was once a land where the only mammal was the bat is now suffering from an imbalance in the animal kingdom. This is causing great problems with the preservation of those unique species, which once roamed freely and without danger over this ancient land. Man has a lot to answer for!

Chapter Fourteen
FIORDLAND

We made Te Anau the centre for our visit to Fiordland and found a motel a little way out of town overlooking the lake from which the town takes its name. The lake, with its three arms penetrating into the mountains, was gouged out by a huge glacier in primeval times. It is thirty-three miles long, about six miles across at its widest and some 1,350 feet deep at its deepest point. After Lake Taupo in the North Island it is the second biggest in the country.

From our patio in this quiet corner we overlooked the empty lake with the densely forested lower slopes of the Stuart Mountains in the distance. Nearby we had a pine tree and in its shelter grew a New Zealand flax, then in bloom. This was a good ringside seat from which to watch the local tuis who waited on the tree until the coast was clear and then flew down to the flax to taste its nectar. We also heard the lovely fluid notes of the bellbird, but though it too feeds on nectar, it seemed too shy to approach our flax, at least when we were about. It was a very restful spot in which to recover at the end of the day from the labours of sightseeing.

The little town of Te Anau has a holiday air about it and a few useful shops, but its most important feature is the Fiordland National Park headquarters. This we found very informative and helped us to orientate ourselves and get some forewarning of all the features we were to see in this great National Park.

Everyone comes here of course with the prime object of seeing Milford Haven and rightly so, but one mustn't overlook the thrill of the seventy-odd mile drive from Te Anau to the Haven. For the first twenty miles the road clings to the western shore of Lake Te Anau, but by now lakes were beginning to be routine and it wasn't until we joined the Eglington river that we began to feel we were entering this great heritage area. The Eglington river, which rises in Lake Fergus and flows into Lake Te Anau after a journey of twenty miles or so, was to be our constant companion, sometimes hidden from view by the ancient beech forest, at others guiding us through the valley between the Earl Mountains to the west and the Livingston Mountains to the east. When we were driving on the flat valley floor, which the Kiwis logically call flats, the gentle wind drove waves through the great swathes of golden grasses which were ripe for haymaking. Then the forest would take over again and we would drive through great stands of trees, mainly Mountain Beech, which has no resemblance to the beech we know at home, having tiny dark green fleshy leaves unlike the larger tender leaves of our native tree.

We were intrigued by the Mirror lakes, which are close to the road and approached by a well maintained path. On a calm day the waters mirror the Earl Mountains opposite and present a unique photo opportunity. When some weeks later my film was developed I couldn't quite place the photos I had taken. But I noticed a slight ripple in the mountains and then the penny dropped. Those photos recorded the reflections of the mountains in the waters of the lake and a zephyr of wind had stirred the surface!

As we left these small lakes, almost ponds in fact, we drove along the Avenue of the Disappearing Mountains. At first we really couldn't understand why the road had acquired this unusual name but then it became obvious. The road stretches straight as an arrow through the forest with mountains ahead and as the road ascends a slight gradient, the mountains seem to loose height until after a while they disappear behind the crest! It's quite fascinating, but magic disappears in its turn as, when one reaches the crest, the mountains suddenly reappear.

Still climbing steadily, we passed Lake Gunn and said our goodbyes to our friendly river as we drove along the shores of Lake Fergus to The Divide, at 1,750 feet the lowest east to west pass in the Southern Alps. Some interesting walks start here, which eventually get above the treeline, but these are for the young and energetic, not us, so we stopped a little further on to enjoy the spectacular views.

Now we began a slow descent between the mountains, often bare of vegetation with occasional patches of snow in those crevasses and ledges sheltered from the sun, and soon we met the Hollyford River, which like the Eglington played a game of hide-and-seek with the road. Then the valley floor flattened out once more at Camera and Lytties Flats as the road wound its way between the mountains towering above us on all sides. By now the bare rocks had taken on a menacing black colour and even the drifts of snow looked dirty with a light covering of black dust and it seemed as if we would run out of road as we approached this great impregnable barrier up ahead. This was the Homer Saddle and at the base of it one could just pick out a black hole piercing the equally black rock, which is the entrance to the tunnel bored through this massive obstacle.

Homer of ancient Greece has nothing to do with this great engineering achievement. The Greeks were fully paid up members of the Flat Earth Society and 'down under' just did not exist for them or Homer! It was an early settler by the name of Harry Homer who found this route to Milford Sound in 1889, but he had to climb over the saddle. It was he who first suggested a tunnel be cut, but a surveyor's report declared it to be "quite useless as a route to Milford". However Harry Homer was a determined man, as one might expect anyone who had laboured to find such a route as this would be! He would not be deterred and prevailed upon the government to send an engineer to look at his proposal. The engineer made his report two years later in 1891 and agreed with Homer that the tunnel was feasible.

Nothing happened for another thirty-eight years but as the depression began to bite in 1929 gangs of labourers with picks, shovels and axes began to cut the road through the valleys and the bush from Te Anau to the Saddle. The men were paid by results on the number of yards completed, and the project was seen to be a useful means of providing work for the unemployed, who would otherwise be getting the dole.

At the end of 1934 the road was almost complete and in July 1935 work began on the tunnel itself, which was to have a gradient of one in ten descending towards the far end. Water was a constant problem in this area, where the annual rainfall is nearly twenty-three feet! About eight thousand gallons an hour flowed into the tunnel they were boring and ran down to the workface where pumps had to be kept working continually to keep the water at bay. The conditions at the workface must have been atrocious and the men must have been constantly wet through. Conditions outside the tunnel were not much better with the ever-plentiful rain in summer and in the short winter days snow and ice added to their misery. But somehow they survived and the work progressed even though disasters struck in 1936 and 1937, when a series of avalanches killed three men and left many injured and much equipment lost or damaged.

In 1940 the men at the workface of the pilot tunnel broke through and saw daylight at last. Now the tunnel had to be enlarged to a width of twenty-seven feet by seventeen feet high, but this work was halted

New Zealand

when the disasters of World War II began to hit the nation and more resources were required for the war effort.

It was not until 1951, six years after victory, that work was resumed, but then within two years it was completed and all that remained was to build the road to the Haven itself.

The Homer Tunnel is not a tunnel we would expect to find on any road in UK with its tarmacked surface and smooth-lined roof and sides. It is rough-hewn and it looks as if it was cut out by pick and shovel, though explosives were used. The road through it is unsealed, water drips from the roof and there is no lighting, though there are ref lectors on the walls here and there. The tunnel is three quarters of a mile long and has this unexpected gradient of one in ten, and despite one's first apprehensions is wide enough for two-way traffic. Unfortunately Harry Homer never saw his tunnel completed and I doubt that he even saw it started, but his idea proved a money-spinner and opened up the unique Milford Sound to the tourist industry. Driving through the tunnel for the first time is quite an experience and when one emerges at the other end the sunlight is dazzling, but the view of the road as it snakes down into the valley is stupendous. From here it is just ten miles to the sound itself.

During our visit to the Glaciers the sun had been more than reticent, but in the fiord it shone for all it was worth from a cloudless blue sky. To come to Milford Sound in the gloom of a foggy rainy day would be a tragedy, but we were lucky and we were able to savour the majestic, serene and powerful scenery in that beautiful light which one gets on a clear summer's day.

I suppose the picture most people remember of Milford is of the Mitre Peak, that great mountain whose sharp and barren summit rises to five and a half thousand feet straight out of the water. It looks like the traditional headgear worn by a Bishop, after which it is named. A smaller tree-clad mountain stands just below it, which is often referred to as the Bishop's footstool. The Mitre Peak and its smaller neighbour feature on most of the postcards and I suspect on most tourists' snapshots. There's a lot more to Milford than the famous Bishop's Mitre, but to see the rest you have to get on the water or into the air.

We decided to go afloat and in the misguided hope that we might be able to get the wind to give us some propulsion for even part of the journey we boarded the Milford Wanderer. She is modelled on the traditional New Zealand sailing scows, whose flat bottoms enabled them to sail around the coast and with the help of the tide, to navigate right up the rivers to supply the settlements far inland.

The Milford Wanderer left the little harbour under engine with sails furled and then there we were in this famous fiord surrounded on nearly all sides by great mountains and cliffs, which were mirrored in the calm waters through which we moved. Here and there huge waterfalls tumbled from great heights into the sea and all save the most vertical of slopes were densely covered by luxuriant forest. Looking down the sound we could see its entrance some fourteen miles away between the steep sides of this primordial glacial valley. The sound is so deep, at around nine hundred feet, that ships cannot anchor in it except in Harrison Cove, where the sealers and whalers used to lie up and the Milford Wanderer now anchors when she does her overnight cruise. Try as one might it is impossible to find words to describe this incredible place. It even defeated Rudyard Kipling, who called it the

'Eighth wonder of the world'. That's probably the best description yet, but it's an interesting thought that the first seven were all man-made, whereas God must have had a hand in this and surely Milford Haven must be at least a thousand times older than the other seven!

We passed the Bowen Falls named after the wife of a former Governor-General and then the Cascades, a mountain range so called because of the water which Cascades without stop down its near vertical slopes. It has also earned the nickname "Elevator Ranges" by the flying fraternity, as the small aeroplanes flying tourists over the sound from the airport at Milford pass close to this massive wall of rock and gain lift from the air currents which rise over it. The little airport at Milford is said to be the busiest in New Zealand, that is on good sunny days! Certainly the planes were busy during our visit, but they were insignificant against this grand scenery and we really hardly noticed them.

Further on, our guide drew our attention to great horizontal channels high up on the cliff. These had been gouged out by harder rock trapped between the glacier and the valley side. Impressive proof, had we needed it, that we were sailing where roughly a hundred and fifty thousand years ago a great glacier had been at work.

I was intrigued by the steep rocky slopes which were so densely forested. The trees are all members of the Podocarp family, who draw their sustenance from the rain and sun and, provided sufficient of these two essentials are available, can grow on barren rock. But how I asked, do they retain a footing, growing as so many do on almost vertical surfaces? Well, I was told, they have a vigorous root system which intertwines with all their neighbours' so that they stay there by mutual support. I found this difficult to believe, but then we started talking about tree avalanches and then I began to comprehend. We could see these long grey vertical scars, growing from a sharp point at the top to a wider base. In earlier times this had been covered by trees, but something, age maybe or storm-force winds or even lengthy heavy rain, had made the top trees lose their foothold and down they came bringing those below with them. Then we began to see other scars, but these were not so grey, in fact some looked decidedly green. Here were mosses and lichens, which had colonised this vacant plot; and soon the seeds of the Podocarp trees will arrive on the wind and root themselves in the receptive moss and lichen. And so the damage done by the avalanche will eventually be eradicated by nature and the forest will finally be restored to its former beauty.

We saw many such tree avalanches in various states of restoration and then it made me think of that great pile of broken trees and rocks on one side with a great gash of a scar on the other side of the road from the Homer tunnel. That too had been a tree avalanche, which occurred a year ago, after nearly twenty inches of rain fell in the preceding twenty- four hours. The road was completely blocked and it took over three weeks to clear a passage through and all the tourists trapped in Milford Sound had to be flown out. But what, I wondered, happened to those like us who came in a hired car? I hope they didn't have to pay rent on a car imprisoned at Milford, but someone had to stand the loss. I suppose the insurers had to pay up but no doubt premiums took another hike!

Although my fellow tourists all seemed to nod wisely when our guide tried to point out both the Elephant and the Lion, two features in the surrounding mountains which have acquired these pet names, I'm sorry to say that I remained blind to these well-versed tourist objects. I was more observant or perhaps luckier when we came to Copper Point and here I felt I really could see the copper ore in the rock.

At Dale Point, the northern coast of the fiord, which till then curves gently from west to south-west, turns sharply north-west. Here the fiord narrows to about six hundred yards between its near vertical sides, and the water is at its shallowest, a mere ninety-odd feet. This is a very typical feature of a fiord, because this is where the glacier finally stopped and melted, leaving behind a great pile of rocks and rubble, an underwater moraine called a step.

A mile or so further out to sea on the southern shore is St Anne Point, where an automatic lighthouse helps the mariner to find the entrance. It was here that John Gruno, the skipper of an early sealing boat found his prayers for salvation answered. He had been caught in a gale and was being driven by the wind towards this unforgiving coast. His death and that of his crew was certain if his boat was thrown against the great mountains he could see ahead, rising almost vertically from the sea. But then when all hope seemed lost, he spied an entrance on his left and turning across the wind he entered the calm waters of this hidden fiord. John Gruno was a Welshman, born in Milford Haven and in thanks for his miraculous escape from death, he named this peaceful haven after his birthplace.

I doubt if John Gruno would notice much had changed in his Sound if he were to sail in once more, that is until he reached Cemetery Point where he may have helped to inter the three early sealers buried there. From there he would see the harbour built for the strange tourist boats, which move without oars or sail and to his right he would notice some enormous winged creatures clawing themselves into the air. But for all that the Sound would be much the same as it has been and hopefully will be for centuries.

There are many other great Sounds in Fiordland, Dusky and Doubtful to name but two, but no other has direct road access. But you can reach Doubtful from the land as we did the very next day.

Doubtful Sound would have remained as inaccessible from the land as Dusky remains to this day had the need for electricity to power a new aluminium smelter at Bluff not been an overriding requirement. Hydroelectric schemes need massive amounts of water that can be dropped onto a turbine from a great height. And some visionary had the idea of using the waters of Lake Manapouri to drive turbines placed deep in the rock beneath the mountains, with the spent water discharged to sea. Lake Manapouri is five hundred and seventy-seven feet above sea level, so if the turbines could be sited just above sea level the power of the water would be colossal. But what would happen to the water once it had driven the turbine? Deep Cove at the inward end of Doubtful Sound is just over six miles away from the western end of the lake and perhaps the spent water could be channelled there.

And so the plan developed. A huge cavern would be excavated just under Leaning Peak in which the turbines would be sited and a long tunnel, the tailrace, bored to take the spent water down to Deep Cove. In 1959 surveys began and by 1962 the exploration shaft had been completed. A workforce of five miners had worked twenty-four hours a day in three eight-hour shifts in wet, cramped and dangerous conditions. Twice the shaft flooded. On the first occasion the inrush of water was quickly stemmed, but on the last the tunnellers had to flee to the surface as the shaft filled with water to a depth of five hundred feet!

Then a road tunnel was dug spiralling down into the rock to gain access to and remove the spoil as a huge cavern was excavated for the turbines. Finally the long tailrace was bored to Deep Cove.

Initially, the equipment needed was brought across Lake Manapouri, but in 1963, work began on a road to link the Powerhouse site with Deep Cove, where ships could be secured alongside to bring machinery and supplies and to remove the spoil from the excavations. A ship was also berthed here to provide accommodation and support.

The whole project was completed in 1971 and electricity began to flow to power the eighth largest aluminium smelter in the world built at Bluff just outside Invercargill.

So now thanks to the Hydroelectric scheme one can visit Doubtful Sound, but it's quite a journey. We arrived at the little village of Manapouri at the eastern end of the lake, where the Walau river joins, to catch our boat. For the next hour or so we cruised the length of the lake enjoying the by now familiar tree-clad, mountain scenery. At West Arm we disembarked and having spent a while in the information centre we boarded our coach, which took us to the power station. Into the side of the rock face we drove and then into a tunnel, which spiralled for a mile or so down into the depths until eventually we arrived at the entrance to the Turbine Hall. Here in this gigantic cavern 364 feet long and 128 feet high the seven huge turbines hummed as they were driven by that great head of water emanating from the lake above. Apart from our small party there was no other living creature present and for a moment the turbines looked like Daleks and I felt as if we were in some great cathedral consecrated to their extra-terrestrial master! But there is no need for people to be here except for routine maintenance, so we left the turbines to their own company and retraced our route back to the glorious fresh air.

Nothing now lay between us and the Sound except New Zealand's steepest and most expensive highway, known as the Wilmot Pass after the man who discovered the route in 1892. It cost something like £20 an inch to build. The workforce struggled with endless rain, snow and rivers of mud as they hacked and tore their way through the forest over gradients as steep as one in five. But it was vital to the scheme and almost ninety thousand tons of material went over the pass during the construction of the power station. The largest single load of 290 tons travelled on a transporter with 140 wheels! It was pulled by a bulldozer and a grader and also pushed by a second bulldozer.

Now Wilmot's Pass is used by the occasional maintenance vehicle and the tourist coach taking parties down to Deep Cove. It is a fine unsealed road, which winds through the wilderness. Here untouched rain forest rolls over the land as far as the eye can see, and in country such as this a colony of the takahe, a handsome flightless bird of the rail family, was found in 1948, that was thought to be extinct.

In bush such as this the smallest of the moa family, those flightless birds which had once roamed in plenty over the land, was probably still alive when the first European sealers made their landfall on the West Coast. A bone of this moa has recently been found with a mark on it, thought to have been produced by a steel tool or implement. The Maoris had no steel until the Europeans came and it is thought that the steel tool used was possibly a nail obtained from the early sealers camping in Dusky Sound. There were twenty-five different species of moas, ranging from the giants, which stood fourteen feet tall, to the small Bush moas at about three feet. The early European settlers heard of these giant birds from the Maoris and when a moa leg bone was found and sent home to England no one would at first believe that such a huge bird could ever have existed.

As we looked over this great expanse of rain forest on which man had made such minimal impact, I wondered how many creatures now thought to be extinct may still in fact be living quietly in that land untrodden by human feet. The chances of finding one must be infinitesimal, but it could just happen.

We had a wonderful opportunity to see some of the many varieties of moss and lichen which grow in the Fiordland National Park. Here by the side of the road where the rock had been left naked as it was cut through, lichen and mosses had colonised the bare surfaces as if it were a tree avalanche. Colours of many hues were represented among the mosses and lichen, from purples to reds, to yellows and amber and of course green as well. Interspersed among the moss and lichen were ferns and here and there a young tree was shooting upwards to stake his claim on the rock.

Shortly afterwards we reached the top of the pass and stopped to take our first view of Deep Cove, some two thousand feet below. Again we were lucky as it was a beautiful clear day and we were able to see the end of the tailrace as it flowed into the cove and the beginnings of Doubtful Sound which seemed to be dwarfed by the massive mountains which hemmed it in from both sides.

At Deep Cove we transferred to our boat and set off down towards the Sound itself. Doubtful Sound is about three times as long as Milford and, some two-thirds of the way from its eastern end, it is dissected by the large Secretary Island, and its northern arm becomes a fjord in its own right called Thompson Sound. Like all the sounds in Fiordland it is very deep except at its entrance. Captain Gook in the Endeavour was the first European to sight Doubtful Sound on Wednesday 14th March 1770. He reports in his log, "At noon we passed a little narrow opening in the land, where there appeared to be a very snug harbour. The land on each side of the entrance to this harbour riseth almost perpendicular from the sea to a very considerable height. This was the reason why I did not attempt to go in with the ship, because I saw clearly that no winds could blow there but what was right in or right out and it certainly would have been highly imprudent of me to have put into a place where we could not have got out but with a wind that we have found lately to blow but one day in a month. I mention this because there were some on board that wanted me to harbour at any rate without the least considering either the present or future consequences". Such were the pressures on a lonely skipper, but Cook's experience and seamanship prevailed and because of his doubts the Sound has ever since been called Doubtful.

In this area where the early sealers hunted the New Zealand Fur Seal almost to the point of extinction, it was lovely to see these animals sunning themselves on the rocks. They are superb swimmers and in their element are like underwater acrobats as they dive and roll with consummate ease. But even on shore they are surprisingly agile and seem able to climb onto rocks several feet above the water level. On land they are territorial and can be aggressive if others come too close but otherwise they lie and soak up the sun. They have been protected by law since 1894, but even today they face many problems including entanglement in discarded fishing nets, being accidentally drowned in the nets of fishing trawlers and swallowing that awful curse of our times, discarded plastic bags, which block their guts. Though the fishermen accuse them of eating valuable stocks of fish, scientists believe that they only eat squid, octopus, lantern fish and barracuda, not the species the fishermen seek.

We also enjoyed seeing the bottle nosed dolphins, who have this lovely trick of jumping out of the water and doing a one hundred and eighty degree turn before diving back into the depths. Whenever we saw one our skipper would increase to his maximum speed and as if mesmerised the dolphins would rush over to play around the bows until once more we reduced speed again. Then as if to celebrate their victory they would move off and execute their wonderful flips. I don't know how much film I wasted trying to capture this wonderful trick of theirs, but I only seemed to photograph the empty sea!

We only had time to motor up the Hall Arm, at the inshore end of the Sound, but the scenery was magnificent and in one respect we thought Doubtful was better than Milford. Whereas in Milford we were in one of a score of tourist boats with tourist planes flying overhead, here in Doubtful we were the only tourist boat afloat, there were no aeroplanes and we shared the Sound with one fisherman quietly tending his lobster pots set on a shelf close inshore. The feeling of isolation and tranquillity was wonderful, and when we went close inshore and switched off our engines we could hear the silence of the wilderness broken only by the liquid notes of a bellbird. It was Sir Edmund Hillary with Sherpa Tensing, the first to climb Everest, who said, "only if you climb and sweat a bit are you entitled to use the wilderness". Yet somehow without expending a drop of sweat, we too had got a glimpse of that magical place and for us our time afloat in Doubtful Sound will always be something to remember.

Chapter Fifteen
A WEE BIT OF THE AULD COUNTRY

DUNEDIN & OTAGO HARBOUR

We were sad to leave our motel overlooking Lake Te Anau, with its view of the distant mountains and our very own f lax bush which attracted the tuis and the bellbirds, but we had planned to visit Dunedin and we had a longish cross-country drive before us. After the grandeur of Fiordland the scenery was bound to be disappointing, but it was varied and pleasant and as I drove I remembered reading Captain Cook's report of the plant we now call f lax, when he first came across it.

"There grows a very broad bladed grass, like f lags of the nature of hemp [used then and since for ropemaking], which might be made into the best cordage or canvas". His prediction was later proved to be true, when early in the nineteenth century on board HMS Dromedary in Sydney harbour, ropes of equal thickness, one made of traditional materials in England and the other made of New Zealand f lax were tested. The English rope parted under a strain of about five tons, whereas the one made of New Zealand f lax carried a load of nearly six tons before it too broke.

The fact that ropes could be made a fifth stronger by the use of this new material made f lax eagerly sought after, and it was largely by bartering f lax for guns that the Maoris managed to arm themselves during the first decades of the nineteenth century. Now ropes can be spun from man-made materials such as nylon, which resist rot and are much stronger still, so the call for flax has diminished, though it is still widespread throughout the country.

A few hours later we were approaching Dunedin on an excellent dual carriageway, which suddenly proclaimed itself to be a motorway and then after a mile or so it reverted to an ordinary road. This chameleon-like behaviour was repeated again for a mile or so until finally the road could make up its mind as to what sort of road it wanted to be! At last it became a busy approach road with more traffic than we had been used to since landing in the South Island.

Dunedin is very different from other New Zealand cities. It has a lovely setting with hills all around it and is located at the head of Otago Harbour, a fourteen-mile-long inlet from the sea, with its own port, Port Chalmers, halfway up on the northern shore. It is the second largest city in the South Island and the fourth in the whole country.

Dunedin is Gaelic for Edinburgh and the Scottish influence of the early settlers who arrived in 1847 in the sailing ships John Wickliffe and Philip Laing is very evident in its character. As the town developed some two-thirds of the population remained staunchly Presbyterian, and so determined were they to retain their Scottish way of life that English settlers were discouraged and vacancies were often advertised with the qualification that "English need not apply". It still seems very Scottish and on George Street is New Zealand's only whisky distillery, where the golden spirit is made from local malted barley and mountain water piped from the Lammerlaw range out to the North West. Here the tallest peak is aptly named Ailsa Crag. Somehow I missed the opportunity to sample this brew from down under, which I am sure is my great loss! But in addition to this very Scottish industry, Dunedin also has one of the great legacies of the Quakers, a chocolate factory, Cadbury's no less. I am always at a loss to understand why it is that all the great chocolate firms in England were started and many are still run by Quaker families and I wondered whether there were many Scottish Quakers in this "New Edinburgh" of the southern hemisphere.

Dick Parsons

There is some good Victorian and Edwardian architecture in Dunedin, the Clocktower building in the University of Otago and the First Church in the centre of town are delightful buildings in the Gothic Revival style. The massive Railway Station and the Police Station are true monuments of the powerful image the Victorians wished to project, but to my eye they look heavy and vulgar.

The town is centred around the Octagon, which is perhaps Dunedin's most unique feature. The design was the work of the Chief Surveyor of the New Zealand Company, a Mr Charles Kettle, who died in the typhoid epidemic which overwhelmed the city in 1862 during, yes, yet another goldrush. A statue of Robert Burns presides over the Octagon, which emphasises the link between the famous Scots poet and this distant Scottish settlement, where his nephew the Reverend Thomas Burns ministered to the spiritual needs of the first settlers.

On the north-west side of this famous eight-sided meeting place, through which the main street passes, stands the Town Hall and St Paul's Cathedral. The former is an imposing building with a fine tower and clearly emphasises the wealth, pride and confidence of the people of this University city. St Paul's Cathedral, despite its prominent position overlooking Robbie Burns, is the Mother Church of the Anglican Diocese of Dunedin. The first Bishop of New Zealand, Bishop Selwyn, visited the area in 1848 and finding a few Anglicans in this new Scottish settlement appointed an Anglican priest to minister to them. The first St Paul's was built in 1863 but in 1900 a legacy was left towards the cost of building a Cathedral on the site. By 1915 additional money had been raised and by 1919 the nave had been completed and consecrated. This first phase was built in a lovely gothic style, with soaring pillars supporting the only stone-vaulted ceiling in the country. With its great height and stained glass windows the nave is both well lit and pleasing to the eye. The chancel is a much later addition, is very modern in style, and as one might expect clashes with the earlier part. It takes the form of a semi-circular sanctuary, and clear glass windows rise from floor to ceiling as a demonstration that the outside world is not shut out nor worship insulated from daily life. This illustrates the progressive ideas of the Anglican Church here, which has been in the forefront of the ordination of women and now has a liberal sprinkling of women priests. In fact I saw from the church notices that the present Bishop of Dunedin is The Right Reverend Bishop Penny Jamieson. Clearly the admonition that "English need not apply" and the unspoken "Women need not apply" have both been banished from this proud city.

Dunedin is also famous for its albatross colony at Otago Peninsula. I had never seen an albatross and having read all six hundred and twenty-seven lines of Samuel Taylor Coleridge's "Rime of the Ancient Mariner", which tells of the dreadful fate which awaits any sailor who harms one of these wonderful birds, I was determined to see one. A few verses of the poem are sufficient to give the gist.

The Ancient Mariner's ship is blown down by gales into the ice of the Southern Ocean:

> The ice was here, the ice was there,
> The ice was all around:
> It crack'd and growl'd and roar'd and howl'd
> Like noises in a swound!

Just when it seemed the ship would be trapped for ever an albatross appears and guides them to open water:

> At length did come an albatross,
> Through the fog it came;
> As if it had been a Christian soul
> We hail'd it in God's name.
>
> It ate the food it ne'er had eat,
> And round and round it flew.
> The ice did split with a thunder-fit;
> The helmsman steer'd us through.

But the albatross continues to eat the rations and despite this magic rescue the Ancient Mariner kills his saviour:

'God save thee, ancient Mariner,
From the fiends that plague thee thus!
Why look'st thou so?' 'With my crossbow
I shot the albatross.'

Now the vengeance of the albatross falls upon them and causes them to be becalmed:

Day after day, day after day,
We stuck, nor breath nor motion;
As idle as a painted ship
Upon a painted ocean.

Water, water, everywhere
And all the boards did shrink
Water, water everywhere
Nor any drop to drink.

After days they see what they think is a boat moving towards them but without any wind to propel it and eventually it hits them:

The boat came closer to the ship
But I nor spake nor stirr'd
The boat came close beneath the ship,
And straight a sound was heard.

Under the water it rumbled on
Still louder and more dread:
It reach'd the ship, it split the bay;
The ship went down like lead.

But the Ancient Mariner survives to warn other sailors to respect the albatross:

> Stunn'd by that loud and dreadful sound,
> Which sky and ocean smote,
> Like one that hath been seven days drown'd
> My body lay af loat;
> But swift as dreams, myself I found
> Within the Pilot's boat.

It is a stirring poem with some well-remembered lines and as we dredged them up from our memories, we drove out along the southern arm of the harbour via Portobello Road and Burns Point as far as Weller's Rock jetty to catch the Monarch, a little wooden ship fifty-five feet long, which was to take us out to Taiaroa Head, where we hoped to see the albatross.

After a little while she hove in sight and when we were on-board she set off for the Head. But almost as she started to move we saw a little blue penguin swimming and diving in the sea close by. This is the smallest penguin in the world and is only about sixteen inches long with a distinctive blue back and head with a white belly and chin. That was a good start, but we were somewhat dismayed when the skipper announced that because of the very light winds the albatross could find it difficult to get airborne so we might not see one in f light!

The Royal albatross is a huge bird with a wing span of eleven feet, a three to four feet long body and a weight of between sixteen and eighteen pounds. It is renowned for its soaring f light, when it uses updrafts and thermals as it glides and only rarely does it f lap its wings for motive power. Albatrosses f ly an estimated 120,000 miles each year at speeds of up to 75 miles per hour. They often regularly circumnavigate the globe and are on the wing sometimes for days on end.

Our skipper had been unduly pessimistic, for suddenly we saw the unmistakable silhouette of one of these great birds gliding over our heads. Their wings droop slightly as if they are too heavy to hold up and they seem to wear a rather mournful expression as they glide effortlessly by. They are a most impressive f lying machine and a joy to watch.

Taiaroa Head is the only place in the world where the Royal albatross nests within easy access of people, and tourists wishing to visit the nesting area are strictly controlled. The Royal albatrosses start to breed when they are eight to ten years old and the current breeding population at the Head is only about eighteen pairs. The breeding cycle begins when the adult birds arrive in September. In October they are busy courting and mating and the eggs are laid sometime in November. The chicks hatch in January to February, which is summertime here and in March the parents leave the chicks, returning now and again to feed them. During summer and autumn the chicks grow and learn to fly and finally in September, as their parents return to start breeding once more, they depart for their lonely life on the oceans. They have a very long natural life; the oldest bird in the colony is over sixty years old!

I felt I could have watched their effortless flight for ages, but there's so much wild life to see at Taiaroa Head. There are, for instance, three different species of shag nesting here. We would probably call them cormorants at home, though of course we do have a shag, but here they are all shags. Cormorants and shags are aquatic diving birds with long necks, a long hooked bill and rather short wings. They are often seen flying low over the surface of the sea, but they also use their wings to 'fly' under water, where they are very manoeuvrable and fish fall easy prey to them. Such good fishermen are they that, when taken from the nest they can be easily trained to fish for their keeper. This was a common practice in mediaeval England, where the Master of the cormorants was one of the officers of the Royal Household. The practice is now obsolete in most of the world, but it is still common in China. A strap is fastened around the bird's neck, so that without impeding its ability to breathe, it prevents it from swallowing its catch.

The three shags which are resident here are the spotted shag, so called because it has a black spot on each of its grey feathers, the rare Stewart Island shag and the smallest of the three, the little shag. The whole area is teeming with bird life, not to mention the New Zealand fur seals, which lie about on the rocky shelves most of the day when not hunting for food. We also saw red-billed gulls very similar in size and shape to our own black headed gulls and the white fronted tern, which like all its cousins dive to catch small shoaling fish just below the surface. They are very dainty birds with long forked tails and narrow swept backed wings and are often called 'sea swallows'. But the other bird we saw, which thrilled me almost as much as the albatross, was the sooty shearwater. Like the albatross, they also have an effortless flight and can be seen gliding at great speed just above the waves and while you're trying to see how they do it they have gone! In New Zealand all members of the shearwater family are also called mutton birds. I had heard this before, but never had an explanation. Apparently the Maoris used to eat the young chicks, which are greasy when cooked, and the settlers who learnt to do likewise thought they tasted like mutton. Hence the name! I was told, though I find it difficult to believe that there are more shearwaters than all other sea birds put together!

In my enthusiasm to capture an albatross on film I probably took a dozen shots. When they were developed most showed a tiny speck in an empty sky, but on one I managed a tolerable close-up which brings back all the excitement of seeing those wonderful birds with their effortless flight.

Taiaroa Head also has an interesting history which goes back to the early 1880s. War between Britain and Russia over Afghanistan, which had for years been called Russia's Gateway to India, appeared to be imminent. The Russian warship Vyestnik, which had an auxiliary engine in addition to a full rig of sails, visited Wellington Harbour in 1886. She was armed with three modern six-inch guns, which so impressed Sir William Jervois, the Governor of New Zealand, that he thought the Russian navy posed a threat to the country. He therefore made plans for the defence of the four main harbours, Wellington, Auckland, Christchurch and Dunedin. The defence of Dunedin was to be conducted from a fort on Taiaroa Head, where eight guns were installed. These were also six-inch guns, but they were modern breech loaders, which were easier and quicker to load than the old muzzle loaders and they could fire a one hundred pound shell over a distance of five miles. They were the new Armstrong Disappearing Gun, the latest thing in gunnery in 1886. They were mounted in pits below ground and when ready to fire were raised above the parapet and fired when the gun's recoil sent the gun back down into the pit for reloading. Thus the gun disappeared from the enemy, who would not have been able to see from where the defence were shooting.

Though they were manned when danger threatened, right up to the end of the 1939-45 war they were never used in anger. Similar guns were fitted by the Americans in Honolulu to protect their new Naval Base at Pearl Harbour, but they too were never fired at an enemy and they were decommissioned after victory in 1945. But here at Taiaroa Head one of these old guns remains in situ in a remarkably well-maintained state and it and the fort are on view for the tourists to wonder at.

During our visit to Dunedin we stayed at a homestay and had a warm welcome and a thoroughly enjoyable stay. Our hostess as might be expected was very Scottish, though she was a third generation Kiwi, and our host was English. Though he had lived in New Zealand for the past fifty-odd years and was very pro-Kiwi, he had never taken out New Zealand citizenship and he told me he has to have his British passport stamped 'resident in New Zealand' before he leaves the country, otherwise he would have difficulty getting back in. "It's too late now to start applying for New Zealand citizenship", he told me, "Anyway I rather like being English!"

I was intrigued as to how he had ended up in Dunedin. He had served in the Royal Navy during the Second World War and in 1945 had been in a ship in the Far East based in Hong Kong. When demobilisation began, men were allowed to complete their demobilisation in any Commonwealth country. At that time our host was twenty and he opted to be demobbed in Australia. His ship had visited Sydney and Auckland during the final stages of the war in the Pacific and when he was finally discharged he made his way to some friends he had made on his earlier visit. They had a small farm in New South Wales and he soon found a job helping them. But once he had saved a few pounds he remembered the girl he had met in Auckland during the war and bought a ticket for New Zealand. Well, he met his girlfriend and they subsequently married and he has lived in New Zealand ever since.

He is a very keen and knowledgeable model railway enthusiast and has a few double-0 gauge engines and some rolling stock, but these remain in a display cabinet. His real passion is the single-0 gauge. Over the years he has built up a big collection, which stands in his garage, where he has a station with sidings built on one side with twin tracks disappearing through an aperture in the wall to run around his garden, before re-entering the garage through another hole to end up in a second station at waist level on the other side. It was a magnificent toy and I could have played trains for hours! He is a London and North Eastern Railway fan so the lovely engines of the old GWR and LMS do not feature in his scheme of things. But he does have a tram and also a London Underground train, which I noticed and admired. He is a Londoner by birth and lived in Harrow where his father had been an Underground train driver, mainly on the Metropolitan line. Sadly he never saw his father again after he joined the Navy and sailed for the Far East, but after his Pa died he went home for a while to see his mother and while in England had a model of the train his father used to drive made and this was the one I had noticed. I'm sure his father would have appreciated this way of remembering him, but he probably wouldn't approve of his son's driving!

We had a very happy time at our homestay in Dunedin and when we left we felt we had made lifelong friends. But before we drove out of town we wanted to see a house in Dunedin which can be compared with some of our smaller National Trust properties. Olveston was the home of the Theomin family and was built between 1904 and 1906. David Theomin was Jewish and came to Dunedin from Bristol during the goldrush. But, like many others, he made a fortune by supplying the gold diggers and with his wealth he built this fine house designed by a London architect. Many of the fittings, such as staircases, balustrades, doors and window frames were made in England and shipped out. The house was called Olveston after a little village to the north of Bristol, where David and his wife Marie used to love picnicking. David Theoman and his family travelled extensively and filled their home with priceless treasures which are still displayed in the house.

They had two children, a daughter and a son who served with the New Zealand Army in France in the First World War. He survived the war, but died a few years later without having any children. When David and Marie died, the house was left to their unmarried daughter Dorothy who lived there without making any changes to it until she died in 1966. She had no heirs and thought at first of leaving the house to the city of Dunedin, but then she worried that they might sell or even demolish it. So wise counsel prevailed and she left it to the people of Dunedin instead, with trustees to oversee its well-being. The house is now open to visitors and is well worth seeing. One becomes used to seeing the simpler buildings and houses of the early settlers, but here one gets a glimpse of the sophistication and elegance which marked the lifestyle of the very rich in this remote former colony.

Dunedin is different. It has a quiet dignity, not often found in this young and thrusting country and it seems to have retained many more of its old buildings, appearing quite happy to be a decade or so behind its contemporaries. We enjoyed our time there.

Chapter Sixteen

MACKENZIE COUNTRY

During our visit to the Glaciers, Mount Cook had remained obdurately shy, but as we left Dunedin in fine sunny weather to visit the Mount Cook National Park our optimism rose as we anticipated our joy at seeing this famous mountain.

We took the coast road to Oamaru, from where the white limestone for the lofty vaulted roof of the Anglican Cathedral at Dunedin had been quarried. Oamaru, unexpectedly for a small town, has many stately white stone buildings, some with Corinthian columns bordering the tree-lined streets. All were built with stone from the local Parkside Quarry, which has supplied stone for other important buildings in the country, such as the Customs House in Wellington and the Roman Catholic Church in Christchurch.

At Oamaru we turned inland and our road followed the course of the Waitaki River as we climbed slowly up towards Omarama, where we joined Highway 8, which ends at the little village in the shadow of the Mountain itself.

We had thought of staying at the Hermitage, a Tourist Corporation Hotel, which is right at the end of the road and though it stands two and a half thousand feet above sea level itself, it is completely overshadowed by the great bulk of Mount Cook which rises nearly ten thousand feet above it. This time fate had decided that our efforts to book a room at the Hermitage would be unsuccessful and had directed us to a farmstay. So when we arrived at the southern end of Lake

Pukaki and had drawn breath after seeing that incredible blue of the water against the golden grasses and the grey snow-clad mountains, we turned right and following the eastern shoreline we eventually found a sign pointing to the sheep station on which we were to stay. We left our smooth tarmacked road and for what seemed an endless twelve miles we bounced over an unsealed track which clung to the water's edge as rabbits ambled nonchalantly across our path and friendly sheep bid us welcome as we drove by.

We were beginning to think that somehow we had missed our way, though that seemed impossible, when suddenly we saw a signpost to direct us and, passing through a gate or two, we finally arrived at a large stone bungalow with pleasant gardens and a superb view of the lake below, the mountain range opposite and to our right low clouds, which hid our shy friend Mount Cook! Clearly the mountain was living up to its Maori name Aoraki, which means the Cloud Piercer!

By now we were beginning to despair of ever seeing the mountain and the following day we retraced our steps down that awful track, and rejoining Highway 80 we drove with an overcast sky above us along the far shore of Lake Pukaki up to the little village below Mount Cook. Still the mountain hid from us, but we had lunch in the Hermitage, packed to the gunwhales with tour parties being shepherded by their guides, and felt grateful that fate had been so kind to us and sent us to our farm!

Though we couldn't see the old Cloud Piercer, there is an atmosphere all of its own in the village, where people seem to talk about little else. Climbing the mountain, hiking round it, flying over it, photographing it or even skiing on it. It is now a great centre for climbing and many mountaineers cut their teeth here before tackling other great mountains. Sir Edmund Hillary, the first man to climb Everest, practised his basic craft on its slopes.

In the mid-1860s the mountain was branded "unclimbable", but in 1873 the Governor of New Zealand offered official aid to anyone who dared to attempt to climb it. For nearly ten years the offer went ignored until in 1882 an Irish clergyman called William Green arrived in New Zealand to climb the mountain he knew only from photographs. He was accompanied by Emil Boss and Ulrich Kaufman, both seasoned climbers of the Swiss Alps. Even reaching the base of the mountain was hazardous. They almost lost their supply wagon crossing the Tasman River, which is fed by one of the huge glaciers which fill the mountain valleys on either side of Mount Cook. Then they had to cut their way through the undergrowth before they could even start climbing. After a few days' hard toil they crossed the large glaciated plateau, which Green named the Linda Glacier. But some twelve hours later, with the summit only about two hundred feet above them, a deep crevasse barred their further progress and in the face of an approaching violent storm they had to turn back. Blasts of fierce wind forced them to hug the steep, weather-worn slope and although the climbers were only a few feet apart they kept losing sight of one another. The descent became a race against time and eventually the storm and darkness overtook them far from their cache of food, forcing them to spend a cold and miserable night sheltering as best they could. Green wrote "We succeeded in finding standing room on a little ledge from which we scraped the snow. It was less than two feet wide and sloped outwards, so that we had to hold on with our hands, as for thousands of feet below there was nothing but steep and crevassed ice slopes"!

After nine hours dawn came and they managed to reach Linda Glacier despite the snow avalanches, triggered by a rapid thaw, which careered past them. But all finally made it safely back to base.

For several years after this almost successful attempt, many others were made but without reaching that elusive summit. In those days, before the era of crampons, progress up the ice could only be made by hacking ladders of spade-size steps up the slopes. What energy that must have required! The development of the crampon was a major breakthrough in the art of climbing, but before this new equipment and the technique of using it became routine, steps still had to be laboriously cut.

But twelve years after William Green and his colleagues had almost made it to the summit, three others were to make the first successful attempt. Christmas Eve 1894 found Tom Fyfe, George Graham and Jack Clarke huddled in a small tent on the upper Hooker Glacier. At

3 a.m. the next day the three left camp and began the steep climb leading towards the north ridge. A deep crevasse between the glacier and the mountain was the next challenge to be overcome and then Green's Saddle, a ridge between the slopes of Mount Dampier and Mount Cook. After a further steep climb up the ice they finally reached the top.

The summit ridge of Mount Cook is about three quarters of a mile long and on both sides great faces of rock and ice plummet over three thousand feet to the valleys below. Below to the east is the mighty Tasman Glacier over seventeen miles long and to the west is the Hooker Glacier. Men on that ridge must feel thoroughly insignificant, though they marvel at the view. But they are at the mercy of the wind which can blow them off into space.

After about thirty minutes on the summit the three began the descent, beset with a rock avalanche, which luckily passed safely by, and the loss of an ice axe, which had to be retrieved by one of the party dangling on the end of a rope some ninety feet below. When at last they reached their base camp, their tent with all their supplies of food, dry clothing and firewood had been buried by the snow wall they had built to act as windbreak. The snow had melted and everything was soaking, so they too had to spend a night on the mountain without food or shelter. But victory had been theirs and their elation saw them through this last trial.

The mountain has been climbed time and time again since that first successful attempt, but now a network of huts has been established to give the climbers a safe refuge in the event of bad weather. However, it is still the greatest climbing challenge in New Zealand and one of the more difficult climbs in the world.

But now Mount Cook is a little smaller, for in the early hours of 14th December 1991 part of the East face fell away in a massive landslide. Luckily no one was killed, though there were climbers nearby at the time and one had been on the face which fell only the day before!

We had no desire to make our own vainglorious attempt on the summit; our only objective was to see it and I'm afraid we had to admit defeat and return to our friendly farm.

Once again on our way home we drove around the southern end of Lake Pukaki, where we stopped on the bridge at the dam beneath us. On one side of the bridge the peaceful waters of the lake pointed the way to that elusive mountain; on the other tumbling waters fed an enormous canal, said to be big enough to float an inter-island ferry! This is part of the Waitaki River Hydroelectric development, which channels the dammed waters of Lakes Ohau, Pukaki and Tekapo down to the coast via Lakes Benmore and Aviemore and finally the river itself. The scheme was first planned in the 1930s and by 1934 the first power station was commissioned at Waitaki. Now there are generators at Tekapo, Benmore and Aviemore, all completed by 1968. Nature has been kind to the electricity generating industry in New Zealand, as the lakes provide an enormous storage of water for the winter months, when the snow-fed rivers are at their lowest level and the demand for electricity is at its greatest.

Rather than tackle the unsealed road back to the farm, we decided to carry on to Tekapo and take another track which leads to the station. The village of Tekapo stands at the southern end of the lake and has an alpine flavour about it, having a little pine forest on the foreshore, wooden buildings and sweeping views across the turquoise lake with the hills and mountains as a magnificent backdrop.

One of the few stone buildings is the little church of the Good Shepherd. Inside the doorway is a notice in beautiful calligraphy, which says "The church was built to the glory of God and as a memorial to the pioneers of the MacKenzie country". The foundation stone was laid by HRH the Duke of Gloucester on 15th January 1935 and seven months later the church was dedicated by the Bishop of Christchurch. It is built of local irregularly shaped stone and originally had a roof of wooden shingles, but these had to be replaced by slate after twenty-odd years. It has no reredos, but instead has a plain clear glass window giving a beautiful view across the lake, which the architect decided could not be bettered by the traditional screen. How right he was. One of the builders, a Mr Rodman, and his fiancée, a Miss Trott, were the first couple to be married in the church. They must surely have had a very joyous wedding.

The high country which is dominated by Mount Cook has been traditionally known as the MacKenzie country almost since Europeans first settled here. It gets its name from a Scot called James MacKenzie, who was accused of being a sheep rustler in the mid-1800s when he ran a flock of stolen sheep, put at about one thousand, in this wild and uninhabited region. He was eventually arrested, convicted of sheep stealing and sentenced to five years' imprisonment. He consistently maintained his innocence and after nine months he was pardoned. But his trial made other pioneers realise the potential of this land and as a result many came to settle in Mackenzie Country.

One of the first to arrive was John McHutcheson, who walked there from Timaru in 1856 with his dog as sole companion. Like many others since, he was captivated by the scenery and wrote "All around me rose the grand everlasting hills whose clear-cut peaks stood out in bold relief against the cloudless sky, while above all loomed the great white throne of the snowy crests beyond. Such were my surroundings as I ate my humble supper that night. Surely never did King or Emperor banquet himself amidst grander surroundings".

From Tekapo village we found the other track back to our sheep station and drove home savouring the scenery of Mackenzie Country. This track, shared by two other stations, is not so badly rutted as the one that skirts Lake Pukaki, but is just as long. This, we learnt later, was the original track to the farm; the other was built in the 1970s when the lake was being dammed for the hydroelectric project.

The present owner of the station is the grandson of the first settler who started running sheep here in the 1860s. He must have been one of those first pioneering settlers who followed in the footsteps of John MacKenzie. The farm originally had about two thousand acres, but when Lake Pukaki was being dammed the level of the lake was raised by an incredible one hundred and fifty feet and as a result nearly half the land was lost together with the original farmhouse and buildings. Our host did receive financial compensation, but for a farmer nothing can replace lost land. All this happened about twenty-five years after he had returned home from the war having been badly injured when piloting a Wellington bomber in the Italian campaign. He had broken his leg badly in a crash in Sicily and had to wait nearly two months for proper hospital treatment, and as a result his leg never really mended. On his return to New Zealand he spent many years helping his father and later running the farm himself, while still hobbling about on crutches! When I admired his level lawn, he told me he knew all about lawns as he had spent much of his convalescence with his mates in the Wirral levelling the tees and working on the fairways of the Hoylake golf course!

But the pioneering spirit of his grandfather lived on in him, and undaunted by the intended flooding of his land and buildings he and his wife salvaged whatever they could. For three or four hours each night after a full day's work on the farm they collected enough of the rounded glacial stones from the lake to build their new house, which they mostly did themselves!

Recently he has had an artificial leg fitted, and so is more mobile now, and he also has his youngest son to help him, who one evening showed us around. Their income depends mainly on the four thousand merino cross sheep they run on their station. Unlike the lowland farms which produce lambs for slaughter, in the high country the sheep are kept for wool and are sheared twice a year. The prime wool comes from the pure bred merinos and is used for making the best woollens, but the wool from merino crossbreeds also sells well and theirs goes mainly to the carpet industry.

We learnt to our surprise that sheep do not have any upper incisors and cannot graze long grass, so to overcome this, sheep farmers usually have some cattle to keep the grass short enough for the sheep. Our host therefore had about one hundred and fifty beef cattle to fatten and to control the grass.

We also saw the shearing shed and the new bungalow they had built themselves for the shearers, and then all the farm machinery and the farm workshop. I found the latter fascinating. Neither our host nor his son had ever received any engineering training, yet they were both competent arc welders and kept all the farm machinery in working order. When their old Bedford lorry finally died on them, they replaced it with a twenty-year-old Commer, but shortly after the purchase the differential went. After a long search they managed to find a replacement rear axle in a scrap yard, though unfortunately it wasn't an exact copy. Nevertheless they managed to modify it and got the lorry working again.

The lorry is a general fetch-and-carry vehicle often used to collect bulk fertiliser, which is normally tipped into the back of the barn. But this lorry was bigger than their old Bedford and they couldn't operate the tipper inside the barn, so the fertiliser ended up in the yard outside. That was a disappointment but quickly cured by fitting a hinge to the roof, so that it could be raised to allow the tipper to be operated in the barn and deposit the fertiliser inside. Ingenuity and a refusal to be beaten are two very apparent attributes on this station.

The lathe was interesting. I had never seen a treadle-operated lathe before and was told that this belonged to his grandfather who started the farm. But Dad had fitted a motor, salvaged from a washing machine, so now it was power-operated. We were also shown a 1940s tractor, still in working order, which they had fitted with a blade between the forward and after wheels. It was only used occasionally to keep the track reasonably graded, but this accounted for our relatively smooth trip back from Tekapo. It seemed to me there was little that couldn't be done in that workshop.

The farm is a long way from civilisation. The Post Office and food store is at Tekapo some fifteen miles away and to visit the nearest doctor, vet and shops requires a twenty-five mile drive. Children have to go away to boarding schools and if the young want to socialise they generally go to Christchurch nearly four hours' drive away. I suppose having been brought up on these lonely farms the isolation becomes a way of life, now happily eased by the telephone and the television, which help to bring farmers and their families more into contact with the wider community. It must still be a lonely life, especially in the winter, yet these people stick at it. I suppose there must be a great feeling of independence, of being your own boss and there must also be a great satisfaction in seeing tangible results from your own hard labours. Not many of us have that!

Most farms the world over have pets, but this one seemed on the verge of overdoing it! The two working dogs, who seemed to love their work shepherding the sheep, were very definitely not pets and were locked up in cages at night, and in the morning could be heard barking and whining in their desire to get on with the job. But besides cats and a pet dog, who was taken on an urgent visit to the vet on the night we arrived, there were other more unusual pets. There was Bambi, a four-week-old fawn and an orphan who had somehow escaped from a venison farm nearby. She had to be given a bottle three or four times a day and we were generally recruited for this task. When she saw the bottle she would come quite happily, but otherwise she was such a sensitive creature and would bolt at the slightest noise or movement. Her whole frame was delicate and graceful, built for speed and agility and there could be no doubt she was the favourite.

On a sheep farm it seemed strange to me that there should be a pet lamb, but Lamby had been rejected by mum, so our kind farmer's wife had rescued her and she too had to be bottle fed. Then there was Molly. She was a wild boar who had wandered into the garden and decided to stay. She had her own wired-off enclosure under the trees where she could root around a bit, but she had her regular rations of damp barley and a few vegetables. Breakfast time was quite a palaver in that household with everyone and every animal eating at different times!

I suppose the farmer's wife, once her children have grown up and left home, has the loneliest life of all on these remote farms, so pets probably play a great part in her life; but I expect that visitors like us do too and our company is probably far more important than the money we bring. Certainly we were made very welcome on the station and we felt we knew the family and their pets as old friends by the time we left.

When we did finally leave, the weather still seemed to be overcast and we had quite given up all hope of ever seeing that elusive summit, but then as we were driving down the track towards Tekapo, miracle of miracles, the sky cleared and there in the distance, we could see this great white mountain looking like an immense piece of icing sugar set upon the grey mountains below it. We could see quite clearly the summit and that long sharp snow-covered ridge, which joins it to its second peak. It was an impressive sight, set as it was against the azure sky, and one that perhaps we appreciated the more because of our many previous unsuccessful attempts to see it.

Now we felt we could leave Mackenzie Country with our mission finally accomplished and head for Christchurch, our next destination.

Chapter Seventeen

CANTERBURY

After finally seeing the summit of Mount Cook and the beautiful mountains and hills surrounding MacKenzie Country, we knew the scenery would seem second-rate on our drive towards Christchurch. And at Burke Pass, which is recognised as the gateway to MacKenzie Country, we said farewell to the high country as the road wound between the hills. A monument erected at the top of the pass records the words of Michael Burke who discovered the pass in 1855. They read "O ye who enter the portals of the Mackenzie to found homes, take the word of a child of the misty gorges and plant trees for your lives thus shall your mountain facings and river f lats be preserved for your children's children and for evermore".

After that last effort by nature to maintain the beauty of our drive, we found ourselves in f lat land almost as far as the eye could see and I began to think how strange it is that this enormous plain, covered by sheep happily grazing the lush grasses, owes its great prosperity to the steam engine and the refrigerator.

The invention of the steam engine and its application to sea transport, firstly in paddle steamers and later in ships driven by propellers, was to bring the produce of New Zealand and Australia onto the world's markets. The Great Britain launched in 1843 by Prince Albert, the Consort of Queen Victoria, was the first propeller-driven ship to cross the Atlantic and in 1858 Brunel's Great Eastern, a monster of 18,914 tons, brought a new dimension to steam power.

She had the new compound engine, which was much more economical with fuel and heralded the possibility of long voyages under steam. This was demonstrated by the Holt Line, when one of their ships completed a non-stop voyage of 8,500 miles from Liverpool to Mauritius.

Though the tea clippers still excited the public's imagination with their annual race home with the new season's tea, such as that of 1866, when the Ariel, Taiping and Serica left Foochow on the same day and berthed in London within a few hours of each other after a voyage of ninety-nine days, the days of sail were already numbered. The real death blow to sail however was the opening of the Suez Canal in 1869, which greatly shortened the steamships' passage to India and the Pacific. The use of steamships was also made more feasible by the provision of coaling ports along the route, making them more profitable as less space was needed for coal and thus more cargo could be carried.

In the Southern Ocean, however, where the distances are enormous, the sailing clippers held their own for a time and ships such as the Cutty Sark and Thermopylae still traded profitably bringing wool from the Antipodes to European markets. In good winds they were fast and could make eighteen knots, and of course the wind was free. But winds can be contrary and passage times varied greatly. The Serica, which in 1866 took only ninety-nine days from Foochow to London, took one hundred and twenty the next year.

Though the steamship might only make eight knots, she could do this on all headings and in all but gale conditions, so her arrival in port could be fairly accurately predicted. Thus steam began to drive sail from the trade routes and by 1870, less than thirty years after the launching of the Great Britain, about sixteen per cent of the world's shipping fleet was steamdriven. Twenty years later it had risen to about forty-five per cent and by the end of the century over sixty per cent of ocean-going ships were propelled by steam.

This great revolution in the propulsion of ships bred not only an expansion in emigration from the old countries, but also permitted the exchange of goods on a vastly increased scale. Thus the trade in wool grew, and it was obvious that a market was developing in England for food to feed the masses who worked in the factories and mines which had been created by the Industrial Revolution. But even the steamship could not get the meat produced in New Zealand and Australia to Britain before it went rotten.

This trade in meat had to await the development and refinement of refrigeration, in which the old discarded East Indiaman, the Edwin Fox, was to play such an important part. But at last in February 1882 the steam ship Dunedin sailed from Port Chalmers, close by the city of Dunedin, with a cargo of frozen lamb. She arrived in the Port of London just ninety-eight days later, when her cargo of one hundred and thirty tons of lamb was sold at a profit of four pence a pound. That works out at four thousand eight hundred and fifty odd pounds sterling, worth perhaps one hundred thousand pounds in today's money!

Henceforth the export of meat and dairy products to England grew spectacularly and a new chain of shops was formed in Britain called

'Home and Colonial' to sell these foodstuffs from New Zealand and other countries of the Empire. New Zealand acquired the reputation for good quality inexpensive lamb, but beef products did not enjoy the same success. Cattle financed by English entrepreneurs could be reared cheaply on the great Argentinian savannas and the beef could be shipped across the Atlantic to Britain. As the time in transit was much shorter transport charges were cheaper and the meat only had to be chilled, thus it kept its flavour and texture better than frozen beef from New Zealand.

Now of course the aeroplane is helping with exports from New Zealand and live sheep are being flown to Moslem countries like Saudi Arabia for ritual slaughter. In UK supermarkets one can now buy all kinds of fruit and vegetables grown in New Zealand, not to mention fish caught in their waters.

Just after passing through Geraldine we turned northwards onto Highway 1. The countryside became much more populated and soon we were entering Ashburton. I have known Ashburton in Devon since I was a boy and it has not changed much since then and is still a delightful little town on the edge of Dartmoor. So we felt we just had to drive around and look at this Kiwi edition. We were surprised how big it is, but it does serve as the commercial, industrial and market centre for the surrounding area. In the 1860s the area was reported as a dry and wind-swept sandy plain, but now irrigation schemes channel water from the nearby rivers and it is one of the most fertile districts in the South Island. From here to Christchurch was a pretty dreary drive, with a lot of traffic on the narrow road, so we were glad when we passed the boundary boards of Christchuch and could start the search for our motel.

In 1848 the Canterbury Association was set up by John Robert Godley, a member of the Board of Directors of the New Zealand Company, with the aim of establishing an Anglican colony in the country. A committee was formed under the Chairmanship of Lord Lyttleton and a Captain Thomas was sent to select a site for the settlement. A little harbour on the northern bank of the inlet that almost cuts the Banks Peninsula off from the mainland was chosen as suitable for development into a port. This was named Port Lyttleton after the Chairman and just behind the hills a site was selected for the new city to be named Christchurch after John Godley's college at Oxford, not after our lovely Hampshire town as I had always supposed. Nor was the river Avon named after the river that flows through our Christchurch, but after a stream in Ayrshire!

Though the city is very flat and laid out on a grid system and the one-way traffic makes it difficult for strangers to find their way around, it looks a very pleasant and agreeable place in which to live. The great landmark is the huge Hagley Park, so big that it is cut in two by a busy road and around which one seems to be able to drive for hours! Hagley Park looks a delightful place to walk, has a golf course and grounds for almost any sport you care to mention and seems to be a jogger's paradise. Through the park the river Avon meanders and tourists hire boats and paddle along its length as it flows round the edge of the city's Botanical Gardens, in which we spent a happy hour or two enjoying the huge collection of plants and trees and the coolness and peace of its green acres.

Christchurch calls itself "The Garden City of New Zealand" and whether or not this is true, it has many public parks and gardens and even has a "City Gardens Tour", which takes the tourist on a visit to selected private gardens as well.

The city is centred on Cathedral Square. The Cathedral, a fine Gothic-style church with a spire climbing one hundred feet into the heavens, was modelled on that beautiful Norman cathedral in Caen. The great pity is that, unlike its English counterparts, it has no lovely Cathedral close to underscore its beauty. Furthermore its position in the centre of a busy square makes it difficult to park. So we were disappointed as we would have liked to have gone inside, but had to admire what we could while the traffic stopped and started on our circuit round the square.

We were flying home the next day so we were short of time and we could only give ourselves an overview of the city and certainly couldn't visit Lyttelton, from which Captain Scott set off in the Terra Nova in 1910 on his fatal expedition to the South Pole. Nor did we have time to visit the volcanic Banks Peninsula, named after Cook's botanical companion, Sir Joseph Banks, nor the original French settlement of Akaroa, which still retains many French names. But luckily for us on our last morning we still had an hour or two to spare after we had returned our hire car, and what else could we do but visit the International Antarctic Centre, which is a stone's throw from airport reception.

New Zealand, the USA and Italy all maintain their Antarctic stations from Christchurch and the hangars for their support aircraft are just across the road from the centre, which was opened quite recently in 1992. The displays and videos are so good that at the end one feels one has been on a lightning tour of Antarctica and seen the great variety of penguins, seals and whales which abound in that frozen land. We in the Northern hemisphere are probably more in tune with the Arctic, which is an ice-covered sea; but the Antarctic is a huge land mass, largely covered by ice, with bare mountains and even an active volcano, Mount Erebus. It is in fact a desert, where snowfalls produce less than two inches of water a year. Yet the huge ice sheet, which covers almost all the land, contains nearly three-quarters of the world's surface fresh water. The ice has been built up over fifteen million years and this enormously thick layer makes Antarctica the highest continent on earth! If all the ice were to melt, sea levels all over the world would rise by two hundred feet or so, drastically altering the face of the planet. The world would also become much warmer as all the ice and snow of Antarctica reflects back into space nearly three-quarters of the solar radiation that reaches the continent.

The great ice glaciers, of which the Lambert Glacier is the world's greatest, being two hundred and fifty miles long by twenty-five miles wide, flow into the sea forming great shelves of ice on the coast line, from which the great icebergs are formed. Part of the Ross Ice Shelf, which is about twice the size of New Zealand, broke off in 1987 to form a massive iceberg, which has been given the poetical name of 'B9'! B9 is no ordinary iceberg, but a giant one hundred miles long and twenty-five miles wide. It is thought to be over seven hundred feet thick, of which only perhaps one hundred and fifty feet is above the surface of the sea.

Scientists tell us that millions of years ago the Antarctic was a really massive continent covered by lush vegetation, home to reptiles and insects. Rivers and lakes were filled with amphibians and large air-breathing fish. In time the vegetation decomposed to form peat and today seams of low grade coal can be found in the Transarctic Mountains. Then some hundred and eighty million years ago this great continent, which has been given the name Gondwana, split up and over the next hundred million years or so the bits drifted apart to form the land masses of the southern hemisphere. Two small chunks drifted away to form New Zealand and took with it primitive plants, insects and birds, some of which were those unique specimens which survive to this day. In one of the displays in this fascinating centre, we could see fossil fern leaves over two hundred million years old! It is by comparing fossils found in Antarctica with those found in New Zealand, or even with the living things, that scientists are able to make deductions and make these statements, which laymen like me find scarcely believable.

It seemed strange that on a visit to this lovely country of New Zealand, we should make this unexpected diversion to that remote and frozen polar land. But thinking about it, it really was very appropriate, for the country we had been exploring had at the start of time been part of that mysterious and frozen continent.

New Zealand

Our time in New Zealand had finally run out and as our jumbo climbed into the sky we made our farewells to this beautiful and fascinating country and vowed that we would return to see those parts we had had to miss. Stewart Island in the South and Mount Egmont and New Plymouth in Taranaki and the Bay of Plenty in the North Island, and many many more.

But though we had said goodbye to New Zealand, that great navigator, Captain James Cook, who put the country on the map was still with us, at least in my thoughts, as we flew to Hawaii for a short break in our long journey home. He too went to the Hawaiian Islands in HMS Resolution with HMS Discovery in company, after his third and last visit to New Zealand. In February 1779 Resolution and Discovery were at anchor in Kealakekua Bay and on the night of the 13th the Hawaiian natives managed to steal a boat from the Discovery. Captain Cook decided that he would have to seize the tribe's leader and hold him hostage until the boat was returned. On the following day he landed with a party of marines to effect his plan, but the natives proved too much for them and the party was forced to retreat to their boats. Cook was the last to retire and as he was nearing his boat he received a blow from behind which felled him. Though he rose again the crowd encircled him and he was overpowered and killed.

So ended the life of one of Britain's great navigators, who had always led from the front and whose maritime discoveries extended the influence of Britain to great areas of the Pacific. Somehow we felt it was right that we should say goodbye to Captain Cook in Hawaii and this was indeed the right place to end our tour of New Zealand.

CHAPTER EIGHTEEN

FINAL THOUGHTS

This has been a personal discovery of this beautiful, mysterious and exciting country. A land seen with eyes that have lived in the reigns of four British Monarchs, three of whom were Emperors of India. They have seen the miseries of World War II and the joy of peace. They were brought up by parents steeped in Victorian tradition and beliefs, when the map of the world seemed mostly red, have lived through the dissolution of Empire and now occasionally get confused by the present names of some former colonies! They have seen the explosion in tourism caused by air travel and the despoiling of many lovely places. In a word they're old. They're not so observant as they used to be and yes, they're probably biased!

So they may portray a different picture from that seen by others, especially the young. Perhaps the screen on which the view is displayed has a few older images in its subconscious, which may taint, modify or even obscure it. And everything one sees is interpreted and analysed by the brain, so what I remember may differ quite radically from that which others recall and of course what one sees is very much influenced by one's interests and activities. So I make no apology for omissions and errors or for a different viewpoint. This is my discovery and my narrative and it records what I saw and my thoughts and reactions!

So what is the final picture that I see when I think of New Zealand? Of course there can't be one. It must be an amalgam of many memories, impressions and experiences.

Man's influence on this ancient land is so recent that on a timescale it is infinitesimal compared with its total lifespan, if that can ever be measured. But by his efforts he has changed the face of nature in great areas of the country and the effects have been colossal.

Though his influence has brought prosperity and a good standard of living to most of the inhabitants, man has however done irretrievable damage to the ancient flora and fauna, which had existed for millions of years. The exploitation of the country's natural resources and the introduction of alien animals have been the main culprits, but I'm afraid to say tourists like me cannot escape blame either, for we are a source of pollution and damage too.

However the Kiwis are now very conscious of their environment and great areas of the land have been proclaimed National Parks; and of course Fiordland is a World Heritage area, so there are controls now in place to protect these unique areas. And although tourism means more hotels, better roads and bigger airports and many more of those Camper Vans, which I suspect cause much more pollution than one might think, it does have a vested interest in retaining and conserving much of the country's heritage in order that the industry will prosper. So hopefully the inevitable increase in tourism will be properly managed and these natural assets not damaged further.

But for the real star attractions like the Glaciers and Fiordland there may come a time, possibly not too far distant, when physical controls on the number of tourists visiting the site may have to be introduced – as they are considering, for instance, in the Lake District in the UK. Milford Sound is a an obvious candidate. There must surely be a finite limit to the number of cars and coaches that can be parked in the reception area at Milford Sound, without further despoiling the area. So it seems to me that there may have to come a time when vehicles will have to wait on the other side of Homer Tunnel for example, until space at Milford is available: this would be an irritating imposition on one's freedom to travel, but tourists have a responsibility not to defile the very thing they have come so far to see.

I suppose I had a preconceived idea of New Zealand as the land of plenty, with bronzed Kiwis working hard but living the good outdoor life to the full. New Zealand's economy has faltered on several occasions before the 1914-18 and 1939-45 wars and very great hardship was suffered. But the wars gave a great boost to the agricultural community, who found that everything they could produce was bought by Great Britain, and this state of affairs continued for the first decade or so of peace, perhaps lulling them into a false sense of security.

But the United Kingdom's entry into the Common Market on 1st January 1973 changed all that and meant Britain could no longer give unrestricted and priority access to its markets for New Zealand produce. This was a bitter blow to the Kiwis, who have never really forgiven the Brits for such a disloyal act after their own great loyalty to Britain in two world wars. One can see clearly how badly they felt about this and the Common Market is a subject best avoided in conversation with them, no matter how friendly they are. One thing that strikes you forcibly is that you hardly ever see on the roads a British-built car, bus or lorry, which was made after the date we joined the Common Market. British vehicles manufactured before 1973 are still frequently seen, but thereafter New Zealand quite rightly realised that her future prosperity lay in finding markets for her products in the countries of the Pacific rim, from whom she now imports the great majority of her manufactured items.

The fear of the consequences of being cut off from their traditional market in UK concentrated their minds and great efforts were called for, and sacrifices made, to implement their new policy of developing different trading partners. But now the farming industry has recovered its confidence and is once again one of the country's greatest earner of foreign currency. Only tourism, I believe, surpasses agriculture with its foreign earnings, and the New Zealand economy is in good shape, with the NZ dollar appreciating against sterling and the US dollar! As a result the Kiwis have a new found feeling of independence and pride in themselves as their trade with their new partners increases.

But my preconceived idea of the Kiwis needs a little fine tuning. They certainly live the outdoor life to the full and they are in a class of their own when it comes to sailing and playing rugger, and often the main stories in the papers seem to be all about sport. They enjoy this macho image and as we all know they invented the bungy jump and the jet boats, which they race up the shallow rivers giving their passengers a thrill as they dodge the rocks. Then there is white water rafting, another dangerous sport, which give the young a physical thrill. But while the Kiwis are busy farming and thrilling the tourist, and putting so much of their energy into the world of sport, the country's industry is slowly being taken over by the Japanese, Taiwanese, the South Koreans and of course the Americans. Other nations – even the British – are involved and for example Stagecoach, which we know as a bus and rail company in UK, is becoming widely seen in New Zealand.

And anyway who are the Kiwis? Certainly the descendants of those settlers from the British Isles regard themselves as Kiwis, but I wonder do the Maoris? And what about the other European settlers, the Greeks, Italians, Yugoslavs and the Dutch to name but a few. And then there are all the Asians, the great number of Polynesians, who probably feel more Maori than Kiwi, the Indians and many others. The latest group to make their home in New Zealand are the Hong Kong Chinese and most of them are the successful businessmen who are now buying large houses, where their children often live on their own, while their parents take a last opportunity to make more money in Hong Kong.

So I keep wanting to shout a message to the Kiwis I like so much, "Wake up, life's got to be fun, but while you're enjoying the good life, there's a whole heap of hard-working entrepreneurs about, who've come in and they're here to make money and acquire control of your business!" I hope they get the message before it's too late, but it's getting late even now.

Then during our short visit I was shaken to learn that this country, which our parents thought of as a land of great opportunity, to which hundreds of thousands came to seek a better way of life, this Eldorado of the South Pacific, with its fertile soil and endless facilities for the good life has one of the highest, if not the greatest, incidence of suicide amongst the young in the world. How can this be? Better qualified people than me have sought an answer to this mystery, but without success. There seems to be no racial divide apparent in the statistics of those who take their own life. Perhaps lack of opportunity to develop one's chosen career, or just plain lack of employment in this modern consumer society may be part of the reason, but in that case, why do eminently successful professional youngsters commit this dreadful act? Maybe competition between the sexes has something to do with it, and no doubt many will blame the stress of modern life, though I believe too much is blamed on stress. Without any shadow of a doubt I was highly stressed in my last job before retirement, but it neither drove me to drink, drugs nor suicide. But then perhaps I was brought up in a tougher regime, where discipline was important and sympathy a rare luxury. However, whatever the reasons for this terrible act, to which so many young Kiwis resort, it is a problem which causes immense concern to all in a land so well blessed by nature. Meanwhile I hope and pray that an answer can be found to this terrible enigma.

But the unhappiness of the Maoris is my greatest concern for this country I have grown to love. Like the Polynesians, from whom they are descended, they seem to have a laid-back attitude to life and often get left behind in the struggle for employment and a reasonable standard of living. Nevertheless, they also have been loyal to the crown and were excellent soldiers in both wars. Obviously there are many in work, but generally in the less well-paid jobs and though there are successful Maori businessmen, they are relatively few. Regrettably, it seems that the great majority of the people who are at the bottom of the pecking order in society, who are poor and disadvantaged and often without jobs are the Maoris.

People say they are idle and don't want to work, but no doubt the same can be said about many Pakehas, some of whom might also be called "layabouts". But I believe such a statement is an over simplification of the issue. The Maoris and Pakehas have exactly the same rights to full-time education, health care and other social benefits, so they should be able to compete against each other on an equal basis when it comes to job seeking. But dare I suggest that perhaps an element of racism comes to the fore when prospective employers hire labour, and that this may possibly explain why the Maoris are so often left behind in this busy country, which itself has to earn its way in the wider world.

The European settlers seem to have bent over backwards to maintain the Maori names, culture and traditions and have been willing to borrow from them, when necessary to give the country an outward sense of unity and identity. The All Blacks chanting the Maori War dance at the start of a match, in order to gain a psychological advantage over their opponents, is a case in point. But is it possible that the efforts made to encourage the Maoris to keep their own culture and traditions has accentuated the difference between the Pakehas and the Maoris, and made both of them feel different and apart?

Maybe with hindsight it might have been better if greater effort had been made to assimilate the Maoris, many of whom have European blood in their veins, into the society of the new developing country.

But whatever should or should not have been done to develop good relations with these people, who after all were in the country some three centuries before the Europeans arrived, there can be no doubt that the Maoris are now beginning to feel hard done by and to resent the affluence and success of the Pakehas.

There can similarly be no doubt that had the Maoris been left alone in their "Land of the Long White Cloud", the country would still be undeveloped and would probably qualify for third world status. It is the energy, enterprise, skill and knowledge of the European settlers which have made New Zealand the successful and wealthy country that it is today.

But the resentment felt by the Maoris is real enough, and in a single act reminiscent of that Maori Chief Hone, who virtually started the first Maori war by cutting down the flagstaff flying the Union Jack at Russell way back in the 1840s, a modern Maori activist recently attacked that lonely pine on One Tree Hill with a chainsaw and had almost succeeded in cutting it down before he was restrained. The tree has fortunately survived, but his act was widely reported by the press in New Zealand and UK and, as intended, his actions have focused widespread attention on Maori feelings of discontent over the way the Treaty of Waitangi has been implemented.

The treaty, you will remember, formally acknowledged by the signatures of the Maori chiefs and the representative of the British

Government, the ceding of sovereignty over the whole country to Queen Victoria, who in turn guaranteed the Maoris the lands, forests, fisheries and other properties they possessed. The Queen was also given the sole right to purchase their lands. All this was given by the Maoris in return for the protection of the Queen and the rights and privileges of British subjects.

The Maoris are now reading the fine print of the treaty and have become aggrieved, amongst other things, about land. Much of the land they own and which is acknowledged to be theirs, was leased to the settlers under a system introduced over a hundred years ago, whereby the tenant has an automatic right in perpetuity to renew the lease on favourable terms. The Maoris want this agreement terminated and to be allowed to negotiate the renewal of the lease on normal commercial terms so that the rent is fixed by the state of the market; otherwise the lease need not be renewed. Many people would say that such a state of affairs could only be seen as perfectly fair and equitable.

The difficult question of land rights is thus once more plaguing the Government and it is very difficult to envisage an answer acceptable to both sides.

A solution has been proposed by the Government, whereby tenants would be compensated for the loss of the perpetual right of renewal, at up to 3 per cent of the unimproved value of the land. This would cost the taxpayer about £2.5 million. But the Maoris are also claiming for the enforced low rents they have had to accept over the last hundred years. The Government has accepted their claim in principle, but the size of the claim in money terms is simply enormous. The Government has therefore sought to impose a limit on the compensation due to the Maoris, in what it calls the "fiscal envelope" of about £160 million.

The Maoris also naturally want to renew the land leases, which are normally renegotiated every twenty-one years, when the present leases expire. But in an attempt to sweeten the pill for the tenants, the Government is proposing that the renewal of leases under the new proposals should be delayed by a further two periods. The Maoris on the other hand see this as an attempt to stop them getting a "fair" rent for their lands for at least another forty-two years and possibly up to sixty-three years!

The fiscal envelope, together with the £2.5 million compensation to the tenants, totals about £163 million and at first sight this does seem a very heavy bill. But if 2 million of the population pay tax, it represents about an extra £82 for each taxpayer in a year, so it doesn't seem such a heavy burden, and the Maoris are determined to seek a better settlement. Meanwhile their feelings of dissatisfaction are running high and they are seeking to gain support for their cause both within the country and overseas.

On Waitangi Day, the anniversary of the signing of the treaty held on 6th February each year, the Governor-General accompanied by Ministers and foreign diplomats attends a commemorative parade in the grounds of the Treaty House at Russell. The Maoris take part and the great Maori War Canoe, manned by eighty Maori warriors is launched and paddles its way at high speed around the bay and a great day is had by all. But in 1995 the unthinkable happened, when Maori activists disrupted the ceremony with a well-organised protest. The Governor- General, Dame Catherine Tizard, the Prime Minister and many of the foreign diplomats were spat at and abused by the Maori protesters, who emphasised their anger by baring their buttocks to the dignitaries.

The disruption of this hallowed ceremony has naturally angered the European population and Mr Bolger, the Prime Minister, has said that because of this inexcusable behaviour, the Government may have to rethink or even abandon this national celebration. But the Maoris feel they have nothing to lose by such demonstrations. Indeed a spokesman for the Maori activists has gone on record as saying that history has shown them they cannot trust the white man, and the Chief of one of the Maori tribes has demanded that the Queen, who was scheduled to visit New Zealand in 1995, should personally travel to his meeting house to apologise for the seizure by the Crown of his tribal land in the last century.

After much agonising and debate Jim Bolger and his Government felt that perhaps an apology might take some of the heat out of the issue and in November 1995 Her Majesty the Queen visited New Zealand and gave a very public royal assent to an Act of apology and compensation. This is the first and only time that an unreserved apology has been made by the crown.

The Waikato Raupatu Claims Settlement Act acknowledges the Crown acted "unjustly" resulting in "a crippling impact" on Maori life and returns 38,000 acres of land in the North Island to the Tainui federation of tribes in the Waikato region. It also gives them compensation of £26 million. This is hopefully one of many similar acts to be drawn up, once the terms of settlement with the many other Maori tribes have been agreed.

Will this bring about a reconciliation between the Maori and Pakeha? An emotional Tainui elder, who was present when the Queen gave the Royal Assent to the Act seemed to think it would and said publicly, "We can't look backward. We need to look forward with the coming together of both your people and our people". He went on to condemn the new strain of Maori extremism saying that patience and perseverance worked, even if the waiting took one hundred and thirty-two years! But the prominent Maori radical, Mike Smith, was sceptical. "This is just a shallow damage control mechanism by the Crown," he said.

It seems that the New Zealand Government has taken its first hesitant step on the long and expensive uphill journey to bring the Maoris in from the cold. Will its stride increase in pace and become more confident? I hope so, for if it falters there's trouble ahead in this beautiful country.

But the Maoris, too, have to be conciliatory. Unfortunately sometimes their desire for the white man to atone for his past sins prevails upon their spirit of conciliation, and there are signs that some still seek "utu". Recently a white New Zealander wanting to take his houseboat up the Whanganui River, where he planned to start a new business, was attacked by stone-throwing Maoris and his way was blocked. They claimed that all rights over the river belonged to them and that they had not been asked nor given their approval for his boat to pass upstream. Another Pakeha, who exports naturo-pathetic medicines, is running into trouble as a Maori claim of absolute authority over some native plants he uses, has been lodged with the Waitangi Tribunal which attempts to interpret the Settlement Acts. Planning consent is another area fraught with polemics between Maori and Pakeha. The press has reported that in some cases the Maori tribes have been persuaded not to lodge objections by means of "consultation" payments. Such "consultation" payments could possibly achieve planning consent for Auckland's ambitious plan to build a new village on the waterfront, with tailor-made facilities for competitors and the media, for New Zealand's defence of the America's Cup sailing trophy in 1999. But first the rival Maori tribes have to resolve their dispute over which has ancestral rights over the area! So inter-tribal rivalry is another obstacle to cooperation and good relations between Pakeha and Maori.

Though a start has now been made in reconciling the differences between Pakeha and Maori, many problems still lie ahead waiting to ensnare them. The most difficult is their perceptions of the other and their different outlooks on life. It may take generations to overcome these two great obstacles, but these two peoples will not live happily side by side until this has been done. I wish the Maoris and the Pakehas every success in their deliberations and negotiations. Neither will gain if this productive land, so well-endowed by nature and developed by its hard-working people, is rent apart once more by racial violence. Two Maori wars are surely enough.

BIBLIOGRAPHY

Anderson, Mona, *The Wonderful World at My Doorstep*

Buck, Peter, *The Coming of the Maori*

Daniel & Baker, *Collins Guide to the Mammals of New Zealand*

Falla, Sibson and Turbott, *New Guide to Birds of New Zealand*

Gillham, Mary, *A Naturalist in New Zealand*

King, Carolyn M., *The Handbook of New Zealand Mammals*

Moore & Irwin, *The Oxford Book of New Zealand Plants*

Reed, A.H. and A.W.(Ed.s), *Captain Cook in New Zealand*

Salmon, J.T., *A Field Guide to the Native Trees of New Zealand*

Sinclair, Keith, *A History Of New Zealand*

New Zealand

A Personal Discovery

Dick Parsons

Two hundred and twenty years after Captain Cook's first tour of New Zealand, Dick Parsons takes us on a more comfortable voyage of discovery round the North and South Islands. He gives us a fascinating insight into the life – human, animal and botanical – of this green and majestic land on the other side of the world.

From 90-mile beach in the far north to Dunedin via the Southern Alps, forests, inlets, glaciers, lakes and islands – even the elusive Mt Cook – are recorded in fine detail; birds, beasts and marine life, plus the impact of man, whether Maori, Scots or English, are described and commented on with fairness and good humour.

Trouble, says the author, lies ahead in the land of the Long White Cloud. A stormy early history, marked by the tainted Treaty of Waitangi, may yet bear poisonous fruit, while new settlers from Asia will turn easygoing New Zealanders further from their European roots and offer them new challenges in the next century. Read, absorb and enjoy – and then see for yourself.

www.ingramcontent.com/pod-product-compliance
Lightning Source LLC
Chambersburg PA
CBHW030321080526
44584CB00012B/660